SHATTERED BY THE DARKNESS

*Putting the Pieces Back Together
After Child Abuse*

Gregory Williams, PhD

Health Communications, Inc.
Deerfield Beach, Florida

www.hcibooks.com

Disclaimer: This book is a memoir that reflects the author's recollections of experiences over time. Some names and characteristics have been changed and some events have been compressed to protect the privacy of certain individuals.

**Library of Congress Cataloging-in-Publication Data
is available through the Library of Congress**

© 2019 Gregory Williams

ISBN-13: 978-07573-2217-4 (Paperback)
ISBN-10: 07573-2217-4 (Paperback)
ISBN-13: 978-07573-2218-1 (ePub)
ISBN-10: 07573-2218-2 (ePub)

All rights reserved. Printed in the United States of America. No part of this publication may be reproduced, stored in a retrieval system, or transmitted in any form or by any means, electronic, mechanical, photocopying, recording, or otherwise, without the written permission of the publisher. HCI, its logos, and marks are trademarks of Health Communications, Inc.

Publisher: Health Communications, Inc.
          3201 S.W. 15th Street
          Deerfield Beach, FL 33442–8190

Cover design by Larissa Hise Henoch
Interior design and formatting by Lawna Patterson Oldfield

Dedicated to

all those that have been abused by the
brutal acts of others.

May this book be the beginning of your
journey into your personal light.

May this book help give you the
courage to share your own
personal story.

You are not alone.

CONTENTS

PREFACE

The nightmare begins with the darkness. The very thing that should bring peace, safety, and rest instead brings horror, pain, and devastation.

Because of the darkness, the nightmare never changes. It plays over and over in my mind. For years the darkness lingered in my heart and head, long after it died.

The darkness is my father.

This is my nightmare.

THE NIGHTMARE
INTO THE DARKNESS

The day begins like every other typical day. I wake up, shower, get dressed, go to work, come home, kiss my wife, have dinner, walk the dog, and then get in my infamous and comfortable recliner to watch a few hours of television. Relax. Calm down. Peace.

The only stress that I want to hear about is whether my favorite singer will last another week on *The Voice*. The only sarcasm I want to experience is the friendly batter back and forth between the judges, Blake Shelton and Adam Levine.

A few snacks later, I begin to doze off and try to make it to the 10 o'clock news. Knowing there's not a chance in the world that I'll ever see the sports report because of my heavy eyelids, I eventually allow my mind to be convinced of something that my body had determined several hours before . . . it's time for bed.

So I walk the dog, brush my teeth, kiss my wife, and crawl in between those wonderful sheets, letting out a huge sigh of relief. Another day is over. Nothing special. Nothing life-changing. Just another day.

But nothing could be further from the truth. This night

will change my life forever. The next few hours will become etched in my memory for years to come.

I lay my head back, close my eyes, and drift off into sleep . . .

The next thing I know, I find myself walking around in the woods. Lost. Dark. Alone. Cold. *What's happening?* I frantically look all around and don't even realize that I am still in my pajamas. I notice a path just ahead that seems to be glistening from the glow of the moonlight. Making sure that I am alone, I start following the winding path.

The leaf-covered trail leads me down a hill. As I make the trek, I notice a small house with a candle burning in the window about two hundred yards away on a hill. I start to pick up the pace, but suddenly the path ends at the entrance of my worst fear . . .

A graveyard. I hate cemeteries during the day, let alone in the middle of the darkest part of the night. I quickly look for another route to the house that bypasses the graveyard, but there is no other route. The only way to the potential end of this horrible night is through the heart of the graveyard.

I start to breathe harder. My heart is pumping loud enough to "wake the dead," and I know I don't want *that* to happen. I break out in a sweat, even though the cool breeze is blowing through my thin pajamas.

Two choices. Turn around and go back into the dark wilderness of the woods or make my way through the cemetery to the house with the candle burning in the window. I take a deep breath, realizing this isn't just another ordinary night.

With every ounce of strength, I pick up my foot and take the first step. Then another and another. "Hmmm, this isn't so bad," I say to myself. "I have this made." The clouds begin to thin out and the moonlight shines brighter on the marble monuments and I squint to read the names and the dates on the larger tombstones.

"What?" I scream aloud (even though I hope no one answers my question).

"It can't be. It just *can't* be!"

I look at the next stone and then the next . . . realizing that I recognize the name and occurrence that is on each of the granite grave markers. Looking for a way out, I quickly try to sidestep them, but my mind can't help but glance at the etched names on the headstones.

My mind is going 100 mph. I begin to look and read the tombstones. Peering in the darkness to make out each name and date, I notice that all of the names are of one person in my life. Not some stranger from an unknown city; this is the name of one person who has caused so many years of hurt, heartache, pain and despair—MY FATHER.

This isn't an ordinary cemetery. This cemetery is the darkest corner of my heart. The blackest, darkest, and deepest part of my spirit. A place where I won't allow anyone or anything to accidentally enter. I don't even visit these places in my soul any more. As I look down and make out the etchings. I see the date that depravity came knocking:

CHRISTMAS 1967

The day my innocence died at the hands of my father.

I quickly look for a way out of the cemetery, but there is no way out. I'm trapped!

All of a sudden, I raise straight up in the bed. Drenched in sweat. The sheets are soaking. Heart racing. Pulse pounding.

Whew! "A nightmare," I say out loud with relief.

"Just a horrible nightmare."

But then I realize that this *isn't* a dream. . . .

I never was asleep.

This isn't a nightmare . . . . this is MY LIFE!

INTRODUCTION

You are just moments away from reading some of the life experiences of my childhood and teenage years of growing up in a rather small and rural country home. These horrific events have been forever etched in my mind and on my heart, even though I tried to keep them hidden and buried for over thirty years.

Before you begin this journey into my past and eventually into my present, I want to encourage you that each person experiences things in life that cause them pain, shame, and embarrassment. However, if you have been subjected to childhood trauma or abuse in any form, the hurt and suffering that you have experienced is exponential. You need to remember that it was not your fault.

For years I felt that I was the cause and blame for all of the abuse that I experienced in my life. That is simply the biggest falsehood ever breathed. But it took me a very long time to understand and believe that. You need to convince yourself of that same truth beginning today.

One word I want to plant deep inside of your mind and your soul as you turn the next page is *resilience*. Resilience to endure pain. Resilience to overcome heartbreak. Resilience to not let broken promises crush you. Resilience to see light in the middle of the darkest times of your life. Resilience to never give up and always keep striving to reach for hope.

J. K. Rowling penned a quote for one of her characters in the Harry Potter series that epitomizes this wonderful wisdom. The character, Sirius Black, is speaking to Harry Potter and telling him that he is not a bad person, just a person that bad things have happened to. Then Sirius utters this life-changing breath of hope: "We've all got both light and dark inside of us. What matters is the part we choose to act on. That's who we really are." What an epiphany! To me, that's what life is all about. The abuses and hurts in your past, along with the many joyous memories that you have had, all woven together form the tapestry called life.

My wish as you read the following pages is that you remember that there is always hope. For those who have endured pain and abuse, you *can* and you eventually *will* step out of the darkness into a light that will help others find their own path through their private darkness. There is always access to light inside of each and every one of us, no matter how black the darkness becomes. Hope never leaves; only our failure to recognize and see it does.

CHAPTER 1

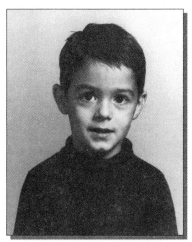

Me, in kindergarten, five years old.

Darkness has many faces and it wears many types of clothes. Business suits, jeans, uniforms, or even medical scrubs.

Darkness is never invited. No one ever sits down and deliberately sends a personal invitation to welcome it.

Darkness always comes as an unwanted visitor and stays longer than it ever should.

Darkness enters in many different ways. Sometimes it arrives quickly and leaves in seconds. Other times it lingers for a few hours or even a few days.

When the night approached the heart of a small child—me—it came in with a vengeance. The unwanted, uninvited visitor brought luggage that would remain not just for an evening or two, but for over a dozen years.

The script was written by a depraved mind full of darkness. The entrance was no accident. It was crafted by a master manipulator and pupeteer. This drama wasn't written for the masses, but for one single small child.

Enter stage left.

Darkness.

CHRISTMAS 1967

There wasn't a day in my childhood that I can remember that I wasn't abused. Living in the country about five miles from a couple of small southern Illinois towns seems to be a perfect place to be raised. A nice, clean, upper middle-class home with two cars in the garage looked from the outside as a storybook setting for a family. The yard was kept meticulously mowed. The backyard was fenced in and surrounded a much-envied swimming pool that many in the late sixties weren't fortunate enough to have. The image was one of a family that was respected, well known, and well liked in the community.

The countryside was covered with oil well pumps, derricks, and what we always called the "eternal flames" burning off the excess gases from the oil pumps at the side of each rig. When you stepped out of our house at night, you would notice the flames from these torches lighting up the skies as far as you could see. There was also the oil smell in the air that we got accustomed to growing up. When friends would visit and ask what that smell was, we always had the same response time after time: "That's money." Many members of my family worked in the oil industry from time to time since it was a major part of the economy back then when the "oil boom" was still active.

As a matter of fact, my mom was crowned the Texaco Oil Company Queen when she was younger and proudly displayed the trophy in our home for years. I remember admiring it as a young child. She always made sure that we were dressed in the best and cleanest clothes and always had our hair combed.

From the outside, everything looked perfect.

I am still shocked that a child can experience over twelve years of daily abuse and it could be so well hidden within the walls of a very "normal" and average-looking home that no one ever recognized it. While I say over twelve years of abuse, please let me clarify. I have no recollection of any memories prior to around four years of age, but once my memories become clear around the four-year mark, then the abuse continues to well past my sixteenth birthday.

Since I have no memory of the first episode, just the beginning of the memories of it happening, part of the deep recesses of my soul fears that I was abused even during the first years of my life, too. But I may be wrong.

My first vivid memory was Christmas 1967. How I remember this is because of my fascination with the infamous Christmas catalogs that my brothers and I would literally wear out by thumbing through and "dog-earring" all the pages containing items on our Christmas wish list.

I remember the cover of the '67 Sears catalog had a cartoon picture of Dennis the Menace, my favorite comic book character at the time. I carried that catalog around with me throughout the holiday season ignoring the Penney's, Montgomery Ward's, and even the Spiegel Christmas catalogs.

A few weeks before Christmas, Dad came into my room and shut the door. My bedroom was probably no different than that of any typical child. I shared the room with my brother who was five years older than me; our eldest brother was ten years older than me and he had his own room down the hallway. We had twin beds and a small dresser between the two beds. On the dresser was a small lamp, a clock, and a few children's books.

Very rarely was the door closed to our room, but when Dad entered in that day, he closed the door behind him. I was sitting in the middle of my bed and he sat on the edge. Dad asked me to show him what I wanted Santa to bring me for Christmas that year. I remember hopping off the bed and grabbing the catalog off the dresser with excitement and quickly opening it up to the numerous worn pages that contained toys that I had in my mind. I could hardly contain my excitement to wake up and see a set of Lincoln Logs under the tree tagged with "For Greg" on the wrapping.

After showing him lots of different toys that I was hoping for, he started explaining to me that only "good boys" got good presents at Christmastime. I remember wondering if I qualified to be on Santa's good list or bad. Dad promised me that the "good boys" did "good things" for their fathers. We sat and talked for a long time. I remember that talk, because dad and I hardly ever talked.

I remember exactly what I was wearing that day. I had on my red plaid flannel pajamas. They were so comfortable. Dad had on his olive green mechanic shirt and pants with his name "Don" embroidered on the left side above the pocket. The pocket of his shirt had his pack of cigarettes and his lighter.

He took out a cigarette from its package and put it in his mouth. Then he handed me his worn silver Zippo lighter and let me try to light it. He would always give us kids a chance to start the lighter with the little wheel to ignite his cigarette.

He took a few long drags off the cigarette and then placed it on the edge of the dresser.

Dad took the catalog and set it on the floor and then picked me up off the bed and placed me directly in front of him. I wondered what he was doing—if this was a game or some type of surprise. But then all of a sudden, he quickly pulled my pajama bottoms down to my ankles and started fondling me. I was frozen with fear. He then unzipped his pants and started fondling himself, too. I stood there for what seemed like hours, but I'm sure it wasn't. He unbuttoned my pajama top and pulled it back. He started rubbing his hands up and down my chest, stomach, and crotch. Over and over.

Through this entire episode, he kept telling me that Santa would be so happy with me and if I told anyone about this, then I wouldn't get any Christmas presents at all, and neither would my two brothers. He insisted that my two older brothers would be so mad at me if that happened.

The look in his eyes was scary as he stared at me throughout the episode. I just stood there wondering what was happening as I watched Dad get more excited and anxious. He finally finished what he was doing and sat down on the edge of the bed. He was breathing hard.

I was a mess. He then picked up my comfortable red plaid flannel pajama bottoms, which became the clean-up towel that he used to wipe himself and me off. He then instructed me to tell Mom that I had an "accident" in my PJs and Dad had to throw them away.

Dad pulled open the dresser and grabbed a t-shirt and pair of shorts and told me to get dressed. He then left the room, leaving the door wide open, and I was just standing there confused. I was thinking to myself, "What just happened?"

Each day after that for the next few weeks, he would use Christmas presents as the tool of discussion to abuse me.

I remember on Christmas Eve when we opened our presents, I was so disappointed that I didn't get anything that was on my list. My brothers and I got toys and games, but I was confused that I still wasn't "good enough" to get the Lincoln Logs or any of the things that Dad promised Santa would bring me. Even on Christmas Eve night, Dad sexually abused me, promising that it wouldn't be too late for the presents to somehow still magically make it under the tree. He abused me again on Christmas night.

I remember being confused, disappointed, and very hurt that I still wasn't good enough for Santa or my dad. As a four-year-old child, I was devastated. Christmas was meant to bring light, joy, gifts, hope, and excitement to a child. But in my case, Christmas of 1967 was the beginning of the darkness, despair, shame, hurt, pain, and disappointment.

The ebb of darkness appeared in my life that Christmas of 1967, and it only was the beginning. From that point on, every night got darker and darker. To this very day when I see Christmas lights, I'm not like everyone else; it reminds me of darkness, not light. Pain, not fun. Sadness, not joy. Darkness inside a four-year-old child's heart and mind that over fifty years later still has the power to dim the brightest string of holiday decorations and cast an eerie shadow on each thought and memory.

CHAPTER 2

Me at my favorite place, my uncle's farm.

*T*he sun starts to fade into the horizon, and the shadows of the early evening begins to cast their mysterious shapes on all the other objects fortunate enough to still experience a few rays of remaining sunlight. Then, as the sun disappears *out of sight, the darkness becomes more evident, and soon nothing can escape the night.*

Even the warmest desert becomes cold in the darkest of the night.

As the night forges on, the darkness becomes a deeper shade of night with no immediate hope of the sunrise to bring light on your face. As a matter of fact, the darkest part of the night seems to be in the early hours after midnight when the entire world seems to be oblivious to what is happening in the darkness.

Darkness has a name. A face. A voice. Darkness has an evil plan to quietly enter a room and destroy its unexpecting prey. When finished, it will quietly leave the blackened room in hopes no one notices the destruction.

Beware . . . darkness can show its ugly face even in the brightest part of the day.

ON MY WAY HOME

The most precious people in my life when I was a child were my aunt and uncle who took care of me during the day while my mom and dad worked. Their presence in my life impacted me more than anyone could ever realize. They lived just a few miles down the country road from my house.

Early each morning, during the week, my parents would drive me down to their house to spend the day and then pick me back up each evening. Their house was filled with great memories of love and acceptance and protection that I never felt in my own home.

My aunt and uncle lived in a nice and quiet home on a corner of two country roads. A simple home with a few cows, a few pigs, some chickens, and a clothesline out back for that special country air-drying. A large garden, a tractor, and several sheds to let a young boy's imagination go wild.

I remember every day when my uncle would come in from working in the oilfields, he would go out to the "old house" and change his work coveralls, and as he would do that, I would play on the old player piano that they had in the back room. Helping my aunt gather eggs from the chicken house or playing a quick game of wiffle ball with my uncle were unforgettable highlights of my childhood. My uncle always seemed to find a way to allow me to hit home run after home run in each of those wiffle ball games that always brought a huge smile to my face. My uncle was never too tired to play another inning with me, no matter how long of a day he had.

I remember many evenings begging not to have to go home when Mom or Dad would arrive to pick me up. I knew that it meant my safe and protective bubble would burst and we were heading back home.

Most of the early mornings when I was being taken to my aunt and uncle's home, I would still be asleep, so things remained peaceful, but going home each afternoon was a completely different experience.

My dad worked as a welder and painter for a company in our hometown that made specialized equipment for large semitrucks. He worked in a hot garage with lots of dirt, sweat, oil and grease. I really only mention this because of the smells and odors that I still can't get out of my mind.

Almost every time that my dad picked me up to go back home, immediately after getting into the car, his hands would be all over me. Many times we'd barely reach the end of my uncle's road before he'd slide his hand down my pants. Even though we only lived a few miles away, that drive seemed like an eternity each and every evening. Many times he would drive extra slow or simply turn a different direction while he fondled me.

We lived near a country lake with a public beach. There was plenty of open spaces for parking, and hardly ever was the lot occupied during that time of the day. Certain days Dad would get so worked up while driving that he would go and park at the lake and unzip his pants so he could use one hand on me and one hand on himself and not have to worry about steering the car.

Up to this point in my childhood, Dad had only done sexual things to me. He touched me. He put his mouth on me. He kissed me everywhere. But the first recollection that I ever had of being forced to actually do things to my dad's body was on these afternoon drives home. I remember so many details about the first time. I will never forget the terrible smells from his body of sweating and working all day in a garage.

Without saying a word, Dad put his hand behind the back of my head and forced me down to his unzipped pants. He would rub my face around his crotch area and then force me to open my mouth as he slid himself in.

I remembered having no clue what I was supposed to do or even what was expected of me. I was never told to do anything. It all happened so fast and unexpectedly. The feeling of being alone during all of this was overwhelming. This was the first time that I couldn't just lay there or stand there. I couldn't ignore the abuse and "fade out." I was expected to do something back. I had a job that I was expected to perform.

Dad started aggressively pulling my head up and down with so much force that it hurt and I was gagging constantly. I remember starting to cry, and he slapped me hard on the back of my head, letting me know that wasn't allowed. Within a few minutes, although it seemed like an hour, I started spitting out something but I had no idea what it was.

Immediately I was screamed at like I had never been screamed at before. Dad pushed me back to the passenger side of the car with tremendous force, and he reached under the driver's seat and grabbed a rag and started cleaning himself off. I will never forget those red mechanic rags. He always had lots of them in his glove box and under the seats for cleanup. I hate those rags even today! I was yelled at and told to never let that happen again. He was so upset with me. He wiped himself off, zipped up his pants, and we drove back to the house. He was fuming, even talking to himself under his breath about how worthless I was and not good for anything. I hated when he talked about how worthless I was. Dad told me that throughout my childhood.

I remember that day like it was yesterday. He was so mad and so disappointed in me.

When we got to the house that afternoon, it was like every afternoon. It was always the same. I would have to help Dad pull off his work boots in the entryway, and he would turn on the television and sit me in front of it while he went and took a shower. He would say the same thing each afternoon: "Sit here and watch TV until your mom gets home." I always did. I never moved. I sat there and wondered what just happened to me and what I did wrong that made him so mad at me.

I remember the loneliness.

I remember the confusion.

I remember staring at the TV and wishing I was somewhere else. Anywhere else. Maybe I could slip off into one of the TV shows and find peace. Mayberry sure looked nice and peaceful. Or maybe even Mayfield didn't look so bad. I would even settle for Gilligan's Island. All I wanted was to be somewhere else. Far away from here. I just wanted to get away from the darkness.

Then Mom would finally arrive at home. My brothers would get home from school or sports practices, and another evening was about to start.

This became my daily routine each afternoon during the week when he picked me up from my aunt and uncle's home. I remember watching down the road, hoping that my mom would be the one to pick me up each day, but that hardly ever happened. It was almost always him.

Day after day.

CHAPTER 3

Me on the school bus, four years old.

The presence of darkness in the world causes normal things to be perceived differently. Sometimes completely differently. It takes what some feel as being normal and changes it.

The very presence of darkness can cause the strong and courageous to become doubtful and fearful. When the heart of innocence has been exposed to the blackest part of the night, it can be forever changed. Forced to be different.

If you put a thriving, growing, and beautiful plant in pitch darkness for days, weeks, and years, the once strong and vibrant plant does what most everything does in pitch darkness.

It slowly begins to die.

THE NIGHTLY VISITS

I t seems very strange, but then again maybe it's not so odd, that I can't remember many things about my childhood when I was four and five years old, but I remember EVERYTHING about each time the abuse happened to me. There seems to be a particular part of my brain's memory that has each instance etched in stone. Normally, this kind of vivid memory is a blessing, but in this case it's a curse because it seems almost impossible to erase those memories from my mind.

The evenings were the worst. My early elementary-school years were filled with nightly visits from Dad in the middle of night. I remember begging to get to stay up later in the evening, because I knew that it would only be a matter of time before he would come to the bedroom. My begging to avoid bedtime wasn't the average child's begging; it was a deep-seated hatred of bedtime. To this day, sleep is not something that I look forward to.

My brother and I shared a bedroom for many years, and we didn't get our own separate rooms until my oldest brother moved out of the house when I was around eight or nine years old. Dad had to be very quiet when he entered the room a few hours after we were sent to bed so as not to wake up my brother who was sleeping on the other side of the room.

Our bedroom was at the end of the hall with Mom and Dad's room just on the other side. There was a hallway light on the wall that had a hook on it, and Mom often hung clothes that needed to be ironed on that hallway light. At night when Mom and Dad had sent us to bed and they were up watching TV, the light from the living room shined down the hall and would cast a shadow from the clothes hanging on the hallway light, projecting a shadow of what looked like a person into our room.

Every evening when I was finally coaxed to bed, I hardly ever fell asleep. I would lie there looking at that shadow on our wall. I was so scared of that figure even though I realized that's all it was, only a shadow. But I knew when the lights went out from the living room and the shadow disappeared, that it would only be a short time before the fictitious child-ish fear would turn into the real horror and presence of my dad standing in front of me at the head of my bed.

My father smoked cigarettes, one right after the other, and I knew each night when the time was drawing near for him to come to my room. I could hear him sitting at the dining-room bar, striking his Zippo lighter to light his last cigarette before coming to me. I still remember the smell of the smoke and the red glowing amber as he took his last drags off of those cigarettes.

All lights were off, except the small night-light in our room. With the cigarette snubbed out in the ashtray, his overpowering darkened figure would be standing there at my bed. My heart would always start racing faster and faster as I anticipated what I just knew was going to happen next. He always did the same thing every time. Night after night, the very same motions.

He would lean over my brother's bed and make sure he was asleep. Then he would approach my side of the room and bend over and say, "Son, it's your dad. Ready?" And he would reach over and slide me to the edge of the bed. Pull down the covers and then slide my pajamas off and put them at the foot of the bed. He always unbuttoned my top and took it off so he didn't ruin it each night.

"Shhhh," he said under his breath. Then he would start fondling me and touching me all over. I remember him always kissing me all over my body, on my face and on my lips. I will never forget the strong smell of his aftershave lotion mixed with the putrid smell of cigarette smoke. He frequently took my hands and put them where he wanted them to go.

If he pushed or thrust too hard and I made a noise, immediately he would slap his hand over my mouth and whisper, "Shhhhh, damn it!" I was afraid to cry or whimper or moan, so I tried to just lie there and let him do whatever he wanted in hopes that it would end soon. I remember many nights he would pick a different part of my body to pleasure himself with. One night it would be my hands, my armpits, the cheeks of my butt, my mouth, or even the back of my knees.

I remember the hairiness of his whiskers bristling against my young skin. The roughness of his hands and the coarseness of his body hair would chafe me. If I was face-down, he frequently jammed his finger inside of me, which caused me to wince in pain. But I knew better than to make a sound. I wasn't allowed to make a sound.

Sometimes he would be very quick and sometimes it would take what seemed like hours. My mind would focus on a certain object in the room that I could see in the glow of the night-light. I wouldn't take my eyes off it. Other times I counted the number of times he would thrust in or on whatever part of my body he was using at the time. Many times I counted the slats on the blinds over and over and over.

I knew the exact number of folds in our bedroom curtains, the exact number of slats on the blinds, and the exact number of stripes on my pillowcase.

I remember one night looking over at my brother's bed, and his eyes were wide open watching what was going on. When his eyes met mine, he quickly closed them, and we never discussed it.

When Dad was finished, he would grab a towel, quickly wipe me off, and quietly leave the room. He never buttoned my shirt back up or put my pajama bottoms back on. I was always left lying there with the covers down at the foot of the bed as his darkened shadow would disappear into the night.

I couldn't get rid of how dirty I felt. Filthy dirty from the stickiness of him not caring to clean me off well enough. The awful smell of his aftershave mixed with the cigarette smoke smell was sickening. To this day, when I smell Aqua Velva, Old Spice, or Wild Country, my mind immediately goes back to my bedroom when I was six, seven and eight years old.

I would lay there wanting to SCREAM, wanting to CRY, wanting to THROW SOMETHING. Wanting to go tell my mom! But I couldn't. I had to try to find a way to stay silent and a way to finally fall asleep.

I was so confused.

So angry.

And so filled with shame.

I was completely alone.

Alone with the memory of the nightly visits from the darkness and becoming very aware that these visits would happen over and over again.

CHAPTER 4

Dad and I at Little League in the summer of 1973.

There are different depths of darkness. When darkness is allowed to enter in and penetrate the heart and the mind, it becomes a horrific inter-

nal darkness that erases the very existence of a conscience.

If the darkness is allowed to take up residency inside that heart, the depth of the blackness will become darker than any mind can ever fathom.

Darkness can become pure evil.

LITTLE LEAGUE SUMMER

One of the things that haunts me the most, even today, is my father's ability to have complete control over me even when he wasn't around. There was a fear instilled inside of me early in my life that I had only one distinct purpose for being alive, and that was to do exactly everything that he asked me to do. It was without question no matter what he wanted from me, I was expected to do it.

I remember a few times pulling away, starting to resist or even crying out in pain, and immediately the kickback was harsh and forceful. My mind and my body learned to cope with the pain and the abuse, no matter what was happening to me at the time.

When I got older, he made his expectations of me distinct and clear each and every time. I never had to guess what he wanted me to do or what his desire was from me at the time. I learned at a very early age not to fight and to simply "block out" the feelings and emotions of what was happening to my body.

There would be many things that I would do to keep my mind off of what was happening to me at the time of each abuse. Just as I had done as a child, I focused on certain items in the room and memorized each characteristic about them. I would also try to count to one hundred and then back down to zero. Other times I would sing songs to myself that my Uncle Ray had taught me as a very young child. It gave me a certain amount of peace during those painful times.

Over the years the idea of just going limp had to be brushed aside, because my father's demands were getting more involved. He would experiment with different parts of my body, trying new things and wanting me to perform different and various acts. He didn't talk too much during the abuse but he would make it very clear with his actions exactly what he was interested in doing or have me do to him.

My father started getting progressively more aggressive during my fourth through sixth grade years. It seemed that his demented desires couldn't be controlled anymore, and on several occasions, my abuse happened at public locations, grocery store parking lots, and in one instance, even in the bathroom of my grade school during a special Thanksgiving school event.

He must have been a master manipulator to everyone around, because not one time was there a situation that was interrupted or questioned. I guess I must have learned to hide the abuse fairly well, too, because not one person in my life ever asked me if I was okay or if there was anything going on that I would like to discuss with them.

Many times I had visible marks on my body, but I made an extra effort to never let anyone see them. I hardly ever missed school and tried just to blend in with the crowd, hoping no one would notice me. Not one teacher ever talked to me about what was normal behavior from people around me. Never did any of my friends talk about that kind of stuff. My own mother never noticed anything going on even though I was being sexually abused each and every day, sometimes twice daily.

As I look back on those years, I honestly thought my life was normal. My dad warned me frequently to never discuss what was happening to me because it was something that should never be brought up, and no one would believe me even if I did. I truly thought that every one of my friends was going through the same thing each night in their own bedrooms. I thought everyone had to go through this with their own fathers. I thought it was normal.

My mom always made sure that my clothes were cleaned and ironed, and I always had the whitest socks and shirts at the school. She always made sure my hair was combed and I looked my best at all times.

So from the outside looking in, it looked as if we had the perfect little family. Nothing stood out to anyone, there were no red flags, and everything seemed as if we were the ultimate upper middle-class home. But behind closed doors, it was a completely different story.

I remember a few times in school that one of the kids would talk about getting hit or spanked at home, but back in the late sixties and early seventies, that wasn't so abnormal. Corporal punishment was used at our grade school by the teachers, and several teachers prided themselves on having the large wooden paddles with holes drilled in them so it would hurt even more when we were being disciplined.

I don't recall ever wanting to tell anyone about what was happening to me. I don't recall ever having anyone inquire about what was a possibility of abuse in the lives of young children. I don't remember anyone teaching our grade school classes about proper touching and improper touching.

Over the years, I learned to keep all of the secrets to myself and to not disappoint my dad. I never wanted him to be disappointed in me. I would do anything that he ever asked me to do, without question. So I kept all the secrets secret.

I think the closest time that I ever thought everyone in the world would notice was when I was in Little League Baseball. The first year was an awesome experience, and I recall loving going to practice and to the games and meeting new friends and learning something new. I picked up on the sport rather quickly and earned my way from the lonely right field position to more of an active and respected spot at second base and then finally to first base.

This was one of the first experiences that I had in my life to go from the country to the city and mingle with the other kids from town. I lived miles out from the town, so I didn't get the opportunity to make friends with the other kids outside of my grade-school friends.

Little League offered me an opportunity to get away from the darkness for a few hours. A chance to be a kid. To have fun. To laugh and be normal.

But not for long.

Somehow my father finagled his way to become the assistant coach of my Little League team during my second year playing. Now he was there at all the practices and games and used that time to continue the sexual abuse on the way to the field or on the way home from the games and practices.

This one instance will forever be burned into my mind, and I frequently still have nightmares about this today. My father showed up early to one of my games and called me from playing catch with my friends. We were right in the middle of a quick game of "hot box" back behind the Little League field.

Dad asked me to come sit next to him on the bleachers, which I did. He had his arm around me, which I didn't think too much of because we were in public. Yet before long, he was rubbing up and down my inner thigh and I was starting to get scared that people were going to notice.

He told me to go to the park bathroom and get ready for the game. I stood up and did what I was told. He followed close behind me. He quickly pushed me into one of the bathroom stalls and proceeded to bend me over the toilet and pull my uniform down to my knees and abuse me. When he was finished, he told me to get cleaned up and not be late for the warmups. He zipped up his pants and left me there. I was a mess.

My white uniform had been stepped on and dragged along the dirty bathroom floor. It took me several minutes to put everything back in order. I knew if my uniform wasn't snow white before the game started that my mom would notice and say something when she showed up to watch me play.

I got myself cleaned up and in perfect order and made it to the ballfield for the warm-up grounders. Dad was already out on the field helping coach the players around.

One this particular day, we were the visiting team, and I was the leadoff batter. I remember it like it was yesterday. The first pitch brushed me back from the plate, and I quickly fell to the ground. So much for the clean uniform. I got up and took three more straight pitches and was told to take first base after ball four was announced by the home plate umpire.

When I arrived at first base, my father was coaching at the coach's box down the first base line. He quickly started brushing off my pants that got dirty from the wild first pitch that knocked me to the ground.

As Dad started to brush my pants off, I screamed, "No!" I immediately thought he was going to pull my pants down again and violate me in front of the entire crowd. My mind started racing 100 MPH, and my pulse was pounding. I was terrified. I had never been that scared in all of my life.

He quickly grabbed my arm and squeezed, whispering, "What in the hell are you doing?"

I came back to my senses in a split second, but never forgot the trauma of what I thought was going to happen to me that day. That was the first and only time that I remember screaming out from my father touching me. I was so embarrassed. No one on the field or in the bleachers had any idea what I was yelling about or even why.

I never felt so alone and confused in my life as I did that late afternoon, on a summer day in front of a bleacher full of parents and kids at the Little League diamond in my own hometown.

CHAPTER 5

Me diving in our pool.

*T*he sense of complete darkness brings a depth of fear and despair that only those who have experienced it can even begin to understand. Being alone in the darkness isn't the main factor that ushers fear in. It is being in the darkness and not being alone that will haunt the hallways of your mind.

Darkness has entered into the room once again, but this time he isn't alone.

This time, darkness brought his friends along.

SUMMER OF 1974

The summer of my tenth year was a summer that forever caused me sleepless nights.

My mother and father were well-known and well liked in our community. They often had friends come over to the house for parties and to enjoy the swimming pool and backyard that they were so proud of.

The parties always went late into the evenings with lots of drinking throughout the night. The guest list on this particular night included a vast variety of friends of theirs who were quite impressive. A local radio personality, a police officer, an attorney from the county court house, and a few coworkers from Mom and Dad's work, along with several others.

One of the things that I actually enjoyed at these parties was that often the guests would throw coins into the deep end of the pool and let me dive in to gather them up. By the time the night was over, I managed to pile up a few stacks of quarters, dimes, and nickels.

During these evenings, my mom would be the hostess, flitting from place to place and never really focusing on me or what I was doing in the pool. Most of the time, she ended up visiting and talking with the other ladies on the back lawn away from the pool and wouldn't notice when I was asked to go to bed. At least I never remember her being the one who would tell me it was time to "call it a night." Dad always decided when it was time for me to get ready to get out of the pool.

On one of the most horrific nights of my life, I was told by my father that it was getting late and it was time for me to get out of the pool and start getting ready for bed. I did exactly what I was told and made my rounds to say good-night to each person and thank them for their coins.

I remember being so happy and rushing to my room to count each and every quarter, dime, and nickel. I counted them over and over again. I remember it was over seven dollars in change. I arranged the money in nice neat stacks on the corner of my little brown dresser as I started to slip off the wet swimming trunks.

The memory is still so fresh and clear and vivid. Some of my memories are in black and white, but this night replays in my mind in bright colors. Why? I'm not sure, but it does. My swimming suit was bright red and my towel was blue with yellow and orange fish on it. The towel was laying at the end of my bed.

As I took the trunks off, I reached for the beach towel to finish drying off before putting on my pajamas. When

I turned around, my dad was standing there and he asked me, "Did you have fun tonight, Son?" I quickly said, "Yes! I got over $7 dollars." He took the towel from me and started drying me off and asked me to turn around.

He took the towel and put it on my head and dried off my damp hair, then he rubbed the towel down my back, my butt, and legs, and then he pushed me face-down on the bed. The next thing I knew, there were three other men in the room.

There was NO DOUBT what was getting ready to happen, and they left the lights on, which was so strange to me. My first thought was to say, "Please turn off the lights," but I dared not say a word. I was so embarrassed to be naked in front of that many people. I wanted the lights off so bad.

While I was facedown on the bed, their hands were all over my body, my back, my butt, and my legs. One man spread my legs apart and started reaching under me and fondling me. Then Dad rolled me over and sat me up on the edge of the bed.

Before I knew it, all three of Dad's friends had unzipped their pants and were putting their privates into my face, taking turns forcing me to put them into my mouth. Dad joined in, too, but he seemed to be more of the ringleader, showing them what to do. There was a smile on my father's face.

In a strange way, my father seemed to enjoy showing me off like a trophy and watching his friends abuse me and get pleasure from forcing themselves on me. All three of them, along with my dad, were taking turns with my mouth, and some were even kissing me, licking me all over while the others were busy doing their own thing.

Dad had a jar of Vaseline, and he opened the lid and took a big scoop full of it in his hands. I remember this clearly because it was the first time he ever used that on me. All the times before, Dad would just use his spit to make parts of me slippery enough for him to do what he had in mind.

I was pushed back onto the bed face up, and he slopped a bunch of the Vaseline all over my privates, and each of the men started humping me, over and over, and taking turns. Then they rolled me over on my stomach and took turns sodomizing me. The pain was excruciating. The worst part wasn't the penetration, but the zipper pull on a couple of the abuser's jeans was scratching and cutting into me. I still have scars on the inside of my thighs today because of that night.

I just wanted to die. I just wanted to get this life over with. This was more than I thought I could handle, and it was beyond my ability to even understand.

The men—all upstanding members of our community— turned me back and forth, over and over, for a long time taking turns in whichever ways they could for what seemed like an hour or so. Finally, each of them finished their course of destruction by ejaculating in my mouth and all over my face and chest.

I still can hear the laughs, the moans, the grunts. I can still smell the cheap cologne and alcohol and body sweat. I can still feel the embarrassment, the shame, the pain, the total confusion. I can still remember praying for them to just hurry up and get it over with.

Finally my prayer was answered. They took my towel and cleaned themselves off, zipped up their pants, and started leaving the room, one by one. Dad took my towel and wiped up the bloody spots on the inside of my legs. He put Vaseline on the cuts and actually looked concerned for a brief moment.

Never saying a word, he kissed me on my forehead, grabbed my towel, and started to leave the room.

He stopped at the door and turned around and glared at me for a long time.

He never said a word.

He turned off the lights.

And he left the room.

For the first time in my life I was relieved to finally be in the dark.

And alone.

CHAPTER 6

How can the experience of darkness be explained to someone that has never been exposed to it in their lives? It cannot.

Darkness isn't something that you enter into or simply control by a flip of a switch. It is a process that begins as a pinhole on the landscape of light and then spreads like a cancer. Day after day, the darkness creeps in and snuffs more and more of the light away.

Like a slow-moving fog that surrounds, invades, and ultimately dominates the entire area in which it was targeting.

Darkness is never satisfied with the presence of even a shred of illumination. It will do anything within its power to eliminate any source of light.

Total obsessive saturation into every part of the heart of innocence.

Unless it's stopped.

But how do you stop the sun from going down and the darkest part of the night to arrive?

You don't.

THE ENTRANCE
OF HATRED

The summer of 1974 was a major downhill experience in my emotional roller coaster of abuse. The group abuse took place two other times that summer. One night it was with six men and another night with four. To this day, I have blocked some of the abuse out of my mind, and I haven't had the inner strength to open the door to those two particular nights. By the time school started in late August, the group abuse ended and never happened again.

During my early teenage years, Mom got a promotion in her office that required her to travel out of state about four to five days a week.

I knew, without a doubt, that once Mom left the house for the work trips, the dam of abuse would quickly burst wide open and cause a path of total destruction.

The stage seemed to be set. It was a perfect environment for my dad's total freedom and access to me. My brothers had both moved out of the house, and now my mom was gone throughout the work week.

Immediately when Mom left for her week-long trips out of town, Dad started requiring me to sleep in the same bed with him. Those nights were filled with constant touching from him along with one or two nightly sessions of sexual abuse.

It's very hard to explain, but these times were some of the hardest. The specific events of the abuse were the same, but the hours of touching before and after throughout each night were ever-present. When he came home from work, he started making me take nightly showers with him.

The evenings were filled with constant kissing, touching, fondling, and cuddling. It was starting to be so repulsive to me and some nights would physically make me sick. I remember going to the bathroom and washing my face and hands over and over again. It seemed that I just couldn't get clean enough.

This became a heavy weight of emotional confusion during those important years of puberty. All of these episodes of abuse were starting to take a toll on my mind. I was so confused since my physical body was developing quickly, and I didn't know how to respond to how my body was changing.

During this time, Dad started making fun of me and saying degrading things about my body and how I was growing into a young man. He would often slap and pull at my genitals and make demeaning comments about how he owned me and I was "his."

Every young teenage boy has questions about their bodies at this important stage of their lives. My confusion was multiplied exponentially because of all the abuse in my life. I simply didn't know what to do about anything. I was lost, confused, and had nowhere to turn to get the help I was so desperately seeking.

The only thing that I knew to do was to continue meeting my father's demands and try to become emotionally dead to what was happening to me physically. I thought blocking out the hours and hours of emotional and sexual abuse would be the best solution. I was so wrong.

I became really good at masking over the internal heartache, the physical pain, and all the emotional damage that was being doled out on me daily. I simply started smiling and pretending that everything was "fine."

The best way to describe how I managed all of this mentally was to become disconnected with what my body was experiencing by trying to disassociate my feelings from actual reality. I was so confused. It wasn't just one sordid act; it was ongoing episodes of abuse that lasted for hours.

I was starting to have girlfriends at school and then coming home after school to experience a completely abnormal relationship with my father. His expectations were continually and progressively getting more and more demanding as each week went by.

I was never allowed to mention girls or if I had a crush on someone. Dad would immediately shut me down and even had a rage of jealousy that would rise up in him. He wanted total and complete control of my emotions and my body at all times.

In our hometown, the teenagers went to the local movie theater on Friday and Saturday nights. I remember my mind trying to grasp the fact that I was starting to be attracted to girls but feeling like I was betraying my father when I would try to hold a girl's hand or nervously put my arm around them.

I remember one of my early teenage crushes. I wrote all over the front of my school notebook, "Karla and Greg," "Greg and Karla," "G.W. + K.S" with little hearts. Innocent and typical things that every kid did, erasing those initials and replacing them with someone else's a few days later.

One late afternoon when Dad got home, I was doing my homework. He walked by the dining-room table where my books were spread out. He stopped and picked up my school notebook and read the etchings that I had written on the front. He screamed, "And just *who* is K.S?" I quickly said, "My girlfriend," with a smile. He grabbed the notebook with one hand and grabbed me by the arm with the other hand and dragged me out of the back door of the house to the burn barrel and threw the notebook in and set it on fire.

"Watch it burn," he yelled. "Watch it burn."

We stood there until it was totally burned up and was nothing but a heap of ashes, blowing in the wind. He looked up at me and forcefully said, "Never again. NEVER!"

He grabbed me by the arm and led me back to the house and into my bedroom. He threw me on the bed and took off his belt and whipped me. When he was finished, he started putting his belt back on and said, "Don't leave this room." He left my room, slamming the door behind him.

This was one of the only days I remember not being sexually abused in the middle of the night.

I lay there crying until morning.

As I laid there, I experienced something inside me that I had never noticed before.

During that endless evening alone and in my room, deep inside me an emotion was unveiling its face.

An emotion that a young teenage boy should never have to deal with.

An emotion that I didn't know existed until that very moment in time . . . .

HATRED.

CHAPTER 7

*D*arkness comes upon the face of the earth each and every night, and our ability to control it is simply outside of our limited skills and talents. This external darkness comes and goes each day with the eternal hope of the light breaking through on the horizon as morning dawns.

But another type of darkness is the self-inflicted layers of black that we place around the chambers of our heart, day after day, similar to lowering the window shades to bring the room to total darkness.

The most damaging darkness occurs when an individual heart seeks a false sense of security in this self-made darkness, not unlike a turtle that hides in its shell, comfortable in the cocoon surrounding it. But staying in the darkness offers a *false sense of peace and only temporary safety. After time goes by, the turtle realizes that no progress can be made until he peeks his head out into the light. Outside circumstances taunt each time the turtle attempts to enter into the world, and the turtle quickly retreats back into what seems to be a safe place.*

Before long, restlessness ensues and daylight becomes a much-wanted heart's desire. The need to break out of the darkened shell becomes a drive that can't be contained. The darkness keeps prodding and poking and humiliating, and anger, frustration, and bitterness eventually reach the peak of the limits and the turtle finally does what is natural and instilled deep down in its heart.

It sticks his head out of the shell . . .

And BITES BACK!

THE HIGH SCHOOL YEARS

The emotions, insecurities, questions, and confusion of a typical teenage boy during his freshman and sophomore years of high school can be an overwhelming time. My mind and body were experiencing all those normal teenage emotions, but also the additional stresses of mental, emotional, sexual, and verbal abuse that had been building up inside of me for over a dozen years.

My early years of high school still involved the daily abuse from my father, but the walls and barriers that I had built emotionally inside my mind and around my heart were starting to crumble all around me. There was an internal pounding that was desperately attempting to break free.

Looking back on these years, I can see how my dad groomed me into exactly what he wanted me to be and how he manipulated my every thought by intimidating me emotionally and physically throughout my life. I didn't make a move, and I didn't have a thought in my mind that didn't include me saying to myself, "What would Dad want me to do?" It was starting to weigh heavily, and the burden was getting harder and harder to carry alone as each day went by.

I had a part-time job at a local restaurant during the evenings after school. I was simply looking for the typical teenager experience of getting to start trying out my wings and finding out who I really was. The first week on the job, I looked out and there he was. My dad started coming in and having coffee for hours each and every evening at my job, just to keep an eye on me.

I remember being so angry and frustrated when I saw him sitting there in the restaurant night after night, laughing and telling jokes with the other locals and calling me over to the table and asking me for a refill. I can still hear his laughter over the crowded room. It still echoes inside my mind.

The emotions bubbling inside of me could best be described as taking a two-liter bottle of soda and dropping it, kicking it around a room, and then picking it up and doing it again and again. The pressure started to build and build until I didn't think I could take it anymore.

During these particular years, I was unable to control my internal anger. I found myself in the bathroom looking in the mirror at myself and hating what I saw in the reflection. The rage and anger would cause me to pull at my hair and start shaking uncontrollably. All I wanted to do was scream.

I couldn't sleep. I couldn't rest. I couldn't find any peace.

I couldn't seem to keep my emotions buried anymore. The pressure was building up inside me, and I honestly thought my heart was going to explode.

On the outside I was smiling and telling everybody that "life was good," but on the inside my heart was pounding and my blood was boiling, and my emotions were growing more and more intense. Suicide was on my mind frequently. It haunted me day and night.

The abuse continued each night even after I turned sixteen. I thought getting my driver's license would be my ticket to freedom, but it wasn't. I would go to school, drive to work, go out with my girlfriend, and then drive home where he would be waiting for me.

I can hardly fathom it even today. I would kiss my girlfriend goodnight and within minutes my father would be kissing me when I walked in the door of the house. I felt so disgusting. So violated. So confused and alone.

Then the day finally came. The pressure was finally too much to bear. My anger couldn't be bottled up any longer.

It was winter of my junior year, and I was at an evening rehearsal with the high school choral group. After the practice, we all went out for pizza at our favorite pizza place in town. It was a nice and normal night with my friends. I took my girlfriend home and starting driving back to my house.

I didn't want to go home but I had no other place to go. I knew what was going to be waiting for me when I got home. My mind was racing. My heart started pounding and my pulse was throbbing.

I remember thinking, over and over, that I could simply push the gas pedal to the floor and crash the car into the small bridge just down the road from our house and kill myself.

I got the car going as fast as I could. The bridge was coming closer and closer in view, and when I approached the bridge, I just couldn't do it. I simply drove over it. I turned the car around and tried it again, but I couldn't bring myself to aim the car at the concrete bridge. After three attempts, I knew that I just didn't have it in me to end my life. I remember thinking to myself, "Geez, I can't even do *that* right."

I went home, drove into the driveway, shut off the car, and walked into the house like I did night after night. I went straight to my room and closed my door, trying to avoid the inevitable. I sat on the edge of my bed and started crying.

I wanted to die. I wanted to just leave this prison of a life. I just wanted out.

It wasn't even five minutes before the door flew open and my dad stood in front of me naked holding his towel in his hand. He said, "Ready, Son?" He approached me without regard that I was sobbing, grabbing me and kissing me. For the first time in my life, I pushed him away with all of my strength.

"Whoa!" he said with a smirk. "What's this?"

I stood up and screamed, "No! No more!"

He looked surprised and then quickly got angry. He came at me again and started pinning me down, taking my clothes off of me and raping me.

At first, I stopped fighting him and started going limp again like always. Closing my eyes, blocking out my mind, and letting it happen to me again.

Yet something inside of me starting building and building and I rolled over and looked up at my dad. I started screaming at the top of my lungs, "I SWEAR TO GOD, I WILL TELL THE WHOLE WORLD WHO YOU REALLY ARE!" He quickly jumped off of me and grabbed his towel, covering himself up, almost like he was embarrassed. Then he left the room, slamming the door behind him.

My heart was still pounding from what had just happened. I started crying again and I screamed as loud as I could to the ceiling, "I hate myself! I hate my life! I just want to die!"

A few minutes later, Dad came into my room with his belt and gave me the worst beating I ever had received in my life. When he was done, he was out of breath, coughing and exhausted. After catching his breath, Dad leaned over me and whispered into my ear, "I love you, Greg." He turned off the lights and left the room, closing the door softly behind him this time.

I remember thinking, "He said 'Greg' and not 'Son.'" That's the first time I could remember that he called me "Greg." I didn't know what that meant, but I will never forget hearing him say that.

Never again did my dad touch me. Never again did my dad abuse me. Never again did my dad whip me or beat me with a belt. Never again.

The nightmare was finally over.

The darkness had left the room for the very last time.

But the darkness that he left inside of me would take over thirty-five years to peel away.

They say that the night is always darkest just before dawn.

But dawn was finally in sight.

CHAPTER 8

Darkness has a way of hiding the ugly reality of destruction in the midst of light. Even on the darkest of nights, the moon has the privilege of reflecting the illumination from the sun that is completely out of sight.

The raw truth about darkness is its ability to penetrate the depths of a person's heart, mind, and soul.

But in reality, even as the moon reflects the sun's light on a cloudless evening, there is the brutal truth that on one side is a surface mirroring light, and on the other side of any given night is a side that is often hidden and forgotten about and never dealt with or visited . . .

The dark side of the moon.

FREEDOM?

F reedom. Finally!
Now what?

I remember feeling a tremendous sense of excitement and exuberance the next few weeks. For months and months, I still couldn't sleep through the night, fearing that the darkness across the hall would once again enter into my room. Nightmares would haunt me continually, and still linger in life even today, almost forty years later.

I felt like a prisoner that was just released on parole after being in prison for sixteen years. Being released without guidance, without wisdom, and without a map to know where to take the next step. I felt lost, confused, and totally bewildered on what to do now that I was free from the abuse.

Dad literally shut me out of his life and would hardly talk to me, look at me, or even acknowledge that I was in the same room with him. I became invisible, and there was little or no communication with him for a very long time even though we lived in the same house.

Probably one of the strangest thoughts I had through-out the process after the abuse was dealing with thoughts of wanting to still receive affirmation from my dad for months and years after. It was as if something deep inside me was missing his presence even if he was abusing me at the time.

I was alone in the aftermath, surrounded by emotional, mental, and psychological damage with nowhere to turn. One of the things that I wish I had during that time in my life was someone that I could talk to. I needed someone that I could share my fears with free of judgment. Unfortunately, I didn't have those kinds of people in my life as a sixteen-year-old.

The nights became increasingly lonely, and even though the abuse wasn't happening to me physically, the abuse emotionally was continuing on through complete neglect and his lack of any kind of acknowledgment of me being alive. It was a complete opposite of what I was accustomed to.

There were so many emotions, so many feelings, so many fears rushing through my mind that I was filled with a sense of helplessness. Helplessness soon blossomed into hopelessness inside of my heart.

The aftermath of damage that sexual abuse has on a person is so deep and complicated that it would take volumes of books to be written to even scrape the surface. It is literally like taking a sledge hammer to a glass heart and slamming the heavy metal right through the very center of it.

The pieces scatter everywhere and can't simply be picked and glued back together. It takes patience and meticulous handling of those shattered emotions for any progress to begin in piecing things back in place.

In my mind, I would often ask myself these questions:

"If I walk out into the light and let the whole world know, what would happen to me?"

"Would anyone believe me?"

"Was this abuse *my* fault? Why didn't I stop it sooner?"

"What would everyone think of me?"

"How would my family and friends view me, and would they ever be able to accept me as a normal person?"

"Would people blame me for this?"

"Am I too damaged to ever be truly loved?"

There were dozens of other questions and doubts that I kept asking myself over and over again inside my mind.

The constant fear of being rejected, of being laughed at, of being labeled a liar was always on my mind. My dad's words would always be played in my mind. "No one will believe you," he told me time and time again. After years of hearing that whispered in my ear, I started acknowledging that as fact. Undisputable fact. I honestly thought no one would believe me. It had been hidden and covered up too well.

After over at least a dozen years of daily sexual abuse, not one person ever approached me about noticing anything wrong! How can a father abuse his son over 4,300 times and no one else gets suspicious? That weighed heavily on my mind, and to be honest, it still does to this day.

Even though the abuse was over, the everlasting effects would ripple through my life for many years to come. I often wonder what kind of person I would be today if I was never abused for all those years.

There was no way to fully answer that question or come close to the truth. The only thing to do was to start sweeping up the pieces of my life and try to make sense out of it all.

But there were so many pieces.

I kept asking myself, "How am I going to do this?"

The answer was painfully obvious—one tiny piece at a time.

CHAPTER 9 ⟶

At the darkest part of the night a tornado of devastating strength rips through the landscape. The total aftermath of destruction isn't discovered until the darkness fades away and the light of the day finally starts shining through.

When the light hits the buildings that have been blown apart because of the monster's strength, the true path of destruction becomes more evident. The damage has been done. The pieces are scattered.

Even though the darkness has disappeared, the presence of the light causes pain because it enables the damage to become visible. Not only to the person the damage has happened to, but it becomes evident to all those around.

Sometimes the overwhelming internal pull to simply cover up the debris up and pretend it never happened is a mounting force. But true freedom isn't found in pretending the storm didn't come in the middle the night.

True freedom is acknowledging the damage and stepping out into the light to start rebuilding and recognizing each and every piece of the blown-apart heart.

And tenderly and patiently putting it back together again.

PUTTING ON
THE MASK

T he years of abuse on a young boy's life can be over-whelming, and I was finding it very difficult to understand everything that happened, and more impor-tantly, *why* everything happened.

The roller coaster of emotions inside my mind vacillated from high anxiety and times of agitation that would quickly peak during bouts of anger that raged within me.

Then, with no warning or notice, I'd feel a huge drop in my life that would bring overwhelming sadness and despair. From one second to the next, the emotional ride would take bends and turns that were confusing and out of my control.

Throughout the rest of my high school years, I remem-ber trying to pretend that my life was absolutely perfect and that nothing was wrong and nothing had ever happened. My inner emotions were trying to scream out to the outside world, but my outer shell would quickly block them from view, and I would just simply bury them deeper in my heart.

I found great peace in a few things back in those days. Music brought me something that I couldn't find in my day-to-day interactions with my school friends. There was something very special about listening to Frank Sinatra sing, "My Way" over and over again on my eight-track tape player in my car.

The words meant something different to me than they probably did to other people. "Now the end is near, so I face the final curtain." I don't know exactly what that song means to most people, but it meant the end was over for me and I would take my life back exactly the way I wanted to, *my way*. It became my personal anthem for freedom.

Writing became another way that I found myself getting some relief from the pressure building up inside of me. I remember finding a few legal pads in the closet of my mom's office, and I would spend hour after hour writing down my thoughts each night. Those pages captured every emotion that I was feeling and every thought that crossed my mind. Before long, those pads were full, and I purchased a couple of notebooks just for my thoughts.

Journaling wasn't a popular concept back then, but I found great comfort in putting everything down on paper. I wasn't concerned about the order or the process; I would just sit down and pour out my heart on paper. I was very explicit on what had happened to me: my feelings, my pain, my fears, my everything. I stored the notebooks in a cardboard box in the back of my closet. Interestingly, after a few years of putting my thoughts on paper, I came home to find that the box had disappeared.

It was my senior year in high school, just before graduation when I noticed that my "box of thoughts" was missing. I never asked Mom or Dad about those notebooks, I didn't dare to, but I sure would pay any price to have those personal pages back today. I remember after each of my parents died, wondering if I would find my journals hidden in the corner of one of their closets. But it didn't happen; the handwritten pages with all of my thoughts as a teenage boy were forever gone. The pages were gone, but the emotions were forever etched in the hidden chambers of my heart.

I continued to persevere, trying to convince myself and everyone around me that life was good and that nothing different was going on inside of me besides the normal teenage thoughts. This was the mid-1970s, and no one talked about sexual abuse, emotional abuse, or anything like that. No one.

It was a different time than what we have now in society. No one taught us about what to do if someone touched you the wrong way. No one explained to us that there were people who would be available to talk to us if we were confused or lonely or scared. I'm not sure that I would have taken the opportunity to share my deepest feelings with anyone at that time anyway, but sexual abuse wasn't discussed, brought up, or taught about.

There are a number of sexual abuse statistics, one of which states that one out of every six boys are sexually abused before they turn the age of eighteen years old. Females experience an even higher rate with one out of every four girls being sexually abused before they turn eighteen.*

One of my goals in writing this book and letting the whole world know about my horror is that people will be more open to talk about their pain. I hope that after reading my story, others would find the courage to face their fears and to discuss their past and deal with it head on.

My biggest mistake after my abuse was to hide it. I thought that if I buried it deep enough that no one would ever find out about it and that it would simply disappear. I was wrong.

During that time, my room—the same room I was abused in night after night—became my sanctuary of safety and protection. Sleeping became something that would rarely happen for long periods of time because of my constant nightmares. I would retreat into my room after school or work and spend hour after hour convincing myself that my life would be fine now that the abuse was over.

The reality is, you can cover things up for a certain

---

* *The American Society for the Positive Care of Children*

amount of time, but then one way or another, it has to be dealt with. The emotions are too powerful to keep hidden for too many years. The ugly face of truth will overpower the masquerade of telling the world that you have lived a perfect and sheltered life.

Acknowledging my abuse was one of the most difficult things I have had to overcome. I used writing as my way of expressing my feelings, but once my box of notebooks went missing, I resorted to the best method that I knew at the time . . . the ever-popular "Bury It and No One Will Ever Know Method."

I took my emotional shovel and dug a deep hole. A hole that I thought would forever be large enough to contain the pain. It worked for a while, but when it finally pushed its way out, it came back with a vengeance.

And it didn't come alone . . . .

It brought companions.

CHAPTER 10 ⟶

On the darkest of nights, lighting a single match can brighten up an entire room. That one flame can eliminate the darkness and bring the safety of light for hours, days, or even years if it's not extinguished.

But if this flame is allowed to burn out of control, it can destroy even the strongest of buildings, with the power to literally wipe out entire neighborhoods. If left unattended or unaddressed, not only can this small fire cause physical damage, it can also cause more internal damage than a person can fathom.

THE STORM
OF RAGE

There wasn't a day that went by during my final years of high school and my early years of college that I wasn't dealing with a growing storm of rage that was continually building up inside of me.

The anger and hostility never showed its face to anyone else. It was always during the darkest of nights after most people were asleep that the torment of rage would expose itself.

It would show up out of nowhere and hit me on nights when I would least expect it. Time after time, I would be lying in my room alone, listening to music or reading a book, or going over some homework and then, BAM! Anger, rage, and extreme frustration would cause me to leap out of my bed in an instant.

The immediate rush of emotion would always lead me to the bathroom to look into the mirror. I remember every time I looked at myself during these times of extreme rage, I didn't recognize myself. It's very hard to explain, but my mind was seeing something different than what my eyes were looking at.

I would stand at the mirror and pull at my hair and slap at my face and grit my teeth so hard that I thought they would literally break off at any time. For hours and hours, the rage would continue on. Some nights would be easier to control than others, but each time the process would be the same. Intense rage. Pulling my hair and hitting at myself. Immediate de-escalation.

I can understand how people resort to self-mutilation and self-cutting when dealing with the internal battles inside their hearts and minds. It is common for survivors of sexual abuse to experience these turbulent times of rage and anger over and over.

Anger is a two-edged sword. While it gave me the courage and strength to fight back against my father after years of abuse, anger had become a damaging force in my life. Anger in itself isn't good or bad, but it needs to be understood and controlled in a safe environment.

Those nights of intense emotions lasted for several years, but eventually faded away with time. Although anger didn't visit that intensely anymore, it still came knocking throughout my early twenties.

At first, my anger became pointed toward the sole person that caused all my pain—my father. For years and years, I dealt with built up anger inside of me toward him.

Anger has a very unique way to remain inside a person

for years like a slow-burning ember and may never ignite into a raging flame until a burst of air brushes over it and then it can quickly set off into a blaze. The devastating damage that uncontrolled anger can have in an abused victim can be overwhelming at times.

Over the years, the internal anger eventually got to me, and in my early twenties, I experienced lots of issues with bleeding ulcers. There is no doubt that my stomach was taking on the issues physically that I was trying to keep locked up inside of me emotionally.

Like fire, anger, when controlled, can be a good thing; a tool that if used properly can be channeled to protect and defend your family, property, and even a country. But also like fire, if it is allowed to flame out of control, it can easily destroy a person's mental state of mind, a family, and an entire home. The key is to control it and allow the emotion a place of safe release.

There are so many ways that anger shows up in sexually abused victims. Lots of times when all of the emotions are bottled up, it can often turn to negative physical and emotional effects and outbursts. If completely internalized, it can lead to bouts with deep depression and even isolation.

It can also lead to serious sleep problems. My nights were filled with countless hours of sleeplessness. I would constantly be walking the floor trying to deal with all the emotions that were going through my mind on any given night. To this day, I only get a few hours of sleep each evening. It's not that I may not need or want more; it's that my mind will simply not slow down enough to relax.

Many sexually abused victims turn to alcohol, illegal drugs, prescription medication, and over-the-counter medication to help them survive those sleepless nights. Over time, many will become addicted just trying to keep their feelings and emotions under control. Some are even trying to find a simple answer to help blot out their hidden hurts and pain.

It is vitally important that the bottled-up anger and emotions find a place to get released. I found that writing my deepest feelings down in a journal helped tremendously. I also find great relief just sitting down at the piano and beating the ivory keys until my fingers are sore.

In a perfect world, just having someone that you can talk to about what you are feeling would be such a tremendous relief. But like me, I didn't have that person that I could trust to discuss those moments with. Or maybe I didn't allow myself to trust anyone that much.

The best advice I ever got through all my years about anger was this: When you feel the anger starting to build up deep inside of you, try to take a big step back and avoid being *reactive,* but then make an attempt to be *proactive.*

Take a moment to try to put everything in proportional perspective. Don't forget to breathe.

The problem with anger is that it is so emotionally charged that it is so simple to lash out at those people around you that you love the most. Try to remember to put everything on pause and allow the emotion to work through its process inside of you. Often my mind is filled with emotions that have nothing to do with the current situation that I am in; they are simply reminding me of something that I endured as a child that brings a tremendous rush of negative feelings.

The more in control I am of my daily emotions, the more I take the reins out of my father's hands in being able to control my every thought and move even though he has been buried for years. It is time for his control over me emotionally to be truly buried in the casket with him and covered up with dirt in a grave so deep that there is no way it can ever be resurrected again.

CHAPTER 11

*W*hen darkness arrives, it's often uninvited.
The night will knock on the door each evening, and
even when it goes unanswered, it will eventually
kick through the door and enter in.

The unwanted visitor looks around the room
and then camps out. Makes itself comfortable and
always stays longer than you wanted it to. It rum-
mages through your things, eats all of your food,
and leaves your house in shambles.

The visitor doesn't talk. It just invades and con-
sumes your thoughts.

Before long, the visitor becomes a friend. A
once uninvited guest becomes a constant resident
that has convinced the owner of the home that you
deserve this. And the only way to survive in the
darkness is by being silent.

THE TERRIBLE
TWINS

There is a set of emotional twins that can reside inside a person's mind. These uninvited guest can take residence inside of your head and stay for far too many years. Who are these unwanted guests? Guilt and shame.

I think two of the biggest reasons that it took me over thirty-five years to let anyone know that I had been abused as a child was because of these two emotions. Guilt and shame don't come alone; they always bring lots of baggage with them. They carry with them some very heavyweight feelings that can keep abuse hidden and secret in the lives of many abuse victims.

I wanted so badly to share everything that was going on in my life throughout my childhood, my teenage years, and even my adulthood. But guilt and shame handcuffed me in a room alone and convinced me not to share my my pain and to try to just handle it all alone.

Throughout my years of growing up, I had a feeling that I was somehow unacceptable because of what had happened to me. In my mind, I thought I would be seen as "damaged goods" and couldn't be seen as normal.

Guilt and shame not only move in to take over the mind of an abused person, but they also try to silence the person and manipulate them into never sharing the experiences with anyone. Because of this silence, I became a prisoner within myself. Over the years, my view that I couldn't be a viable contributing person in society caused my personality to change. Even though I pretended to be "fine and dandy" to the world, inside I was decaying and serving my self-imposed prison time behind the iron bars of guilt and shame.

Guilt and shame prevented me from getting too close to people, both physically and emotionally. I just knew in my mind that they would eventually hurt me or try to use me for their own pleasure or gain. I would internally be begging for a friendship but then quickly push people away because of my fears.

After years of feeling guilt and shame, I believed that hiding my real feelings about my real life and about my real past was the only way to deal with other people.

During my freshman year in college, I had a roommate that I will never forget. We quickly became good friends and spent lots of nights talking about life and the challenges of being a rookie student in a college hundreds of miles away from home.

One night we got into a deep discussion about our parents. He shared with me about his childhood and how special his parents were and the wonderful way they brought him up. He then turned the conversation around and directed it at me.

He said, "So, tell me about your mom and dad."

I started in immediately with the normal response. "My childhood was great! I have wonderful parents."

Steve stopped and said, "I hear the words coming out of your mouth, but your facial expression doesn't match what you are saying."

I quickly gave an awkward answer to try to cover up all the years of emotions and abuse.

He said, "Now *really* tell me about your mom and dad."

I went straight to my mom and her career and our beautiful house and all the things she bought me. But it wasn't covering up the truth like normal. My real emotions were bleeding through and my roommate could see that I was simply not answering his question.

"Greg," Steve said. "What's wrong?" I immediately started crying and sobbed for about ten minutes. I looked up at him and he had the infamous "deer in the headlights" look on his face. He asked, "Did I say something wrong?"

After taking a very deep breath, I said, "My dad was pure evil." And I started sharing very briefly about my childhood. I hardly went into any details.

The look on Steve's face was shocking. Here I was on the edge of telling someone for the very first time about all of these years of sexual abuse and he looked totally disgusted. He pushed himself back in his dorm chair and gave me the "holier than thou" attitude and said, "I don't want to hear that junk!"

I was appalled! I was shocked! I was so embarrassed that I was ready to tell him the whole story and his response was as if I was repulsive to him. From that moment on, our friendship was splintered. We never had deep discussions again and he always put me at a distance. It was as if I had a communicable disease.

Inside my mind there was a song playing over and over. A song of guilt and shame and embarrassment. I remember taking a long walk around campus the next morning and blaming myself for being so stupid to let anyone know my real past. I kept mentally kicking myself and asking myself, "How could I be *so* stupid?"

About a month later, Steve put in a request for a different roommate and I ended up spending the rest of my freshman year in a dorm room alone. Alone again.

From that moment on, I convinced myself that silence would be my key to real freedom.

The words of Simon and Garfunkel's "The Sound of Silence" started becoming a reality to me:

"Hello darkness, my old friend
I've come to talk with you again..."

I listened to that song over and over, convincing myself that the only real way to survive was to remain silent.

I was so wrong.

Real freedom was in serving the eviction notice to those two unwanted guests: guilt and shame.

Real freedom was in finding someone to talk to that would not only hear what I was saying but would listen with an open heart and accept me without judgment.

I knew what I needed to do. While I emotionally typed up the eviction notice, it took me another thirty years before I served the papers.

The uninvited guests stayed for over three more decades rent free.

It costs them nothing to reside there . . . but it cost me everything.

CHAPTER 12

The darkness of any given evening is controlled and limited by the hours on a clock. Physical darkness can't stay any longer than the sun allows it to. Every morning the light slowly breaks through and takes back the control, forcing the darkness to retreat.

Night after night, just when the darkness thinks it has total power, the morning takes back its control.

The sun has total power *over the darkness.*

But sometimes the darkness isn't satisfied to wait until the next evening to arrive. It can rear its ugly head by bringing some very black clouds that try to block out the rays of the noonday sun.

There is also a phenomenon that happens periodically during certain times of the year that somehow slip in during the brightest part of the day.

An eclipse.

For a brief time, an eclipse has the power to take out all of the light from the day.

But it doesn't last long.

The sun will eventually shine back through and put darkness in its proper place.

STAYING GROUNDED

I have often wondered what type of person I would be today if I had a normal childhood. I guess in the grand scheme of things, no one has a normal childhood, do they? Even though my life has been free of abuse for almost forty years, there isn't a day that goes by during which the bad memories don't reappear.

The affects of being abused throughout my childhood are too numerous to mention, but there are a few that I know I have to battle with each and every day. Of course, there are days that go smoothly emotionally and I hardly even think about the bad times. But there isn't a week that goes by that my mind, emotions, and nerves aren't being manipulated by the past.

Even though my father has been dead for over sixteen years now, he still has a way to reach out from his grave and influence my thoughts and emotions at any given time of the day. No matter how hard I try to push the thoughts out of my mind and lock the door behind them, he can somehow pick the lock and slowly creep in.

The emotional life that I experience, along with thousands of other abused victims, can be very complicated at times. The rush of feelings, emotions, and thoughts at any given time of the day can often blindside me when I least expect it.

The other day I was making a couple of pots of coffee and as I was pouring in the water for the second pot, I quickly realized that I still hadn't placed an empty pot underneath the dripper and the coffee was spilling over and running everywhere.

I looked around and couldn't find the extra empty decanter and there was nothing I could do to stop the coffee from going everywhere on the counter and onto the floor. I couldn't stop the flow and it kept streaming out more and more.

Right there in the middle of the early morning, my mind recognized that this was exactly how my mind and my heart feel on some days. The flood of emotions starts brewing deep inside of my and then spills out. But many days there aren't enough containers to catch all the rush of emotions and it just pours everywhere on those people in my life.

No matter how hard I try to look for another spot for the emotions to go to, it simply isn't enough. They over-flow everywhere.

Sometimes burning them unnecessarily.

Sometimes soaking them undeservingly.

Sometimes just making a mess out of things during a typical morning routine.

I never ask for it. I never plan for it. The emotions just spill over.

Some days I quickly recover and find another pot for the feelings to pour into and the damage is minimal. But to be honest, some days no matter how hard I try, the emotions can't be stopped and they ruin everything around me. There is a helplessness that ensues on those days. The overwhelming stream of emotions takes its toll on the mind over the years.

There are so many coping mechanisms that I have tried to engage during those emotional rushes. Some were very successful throughout the years and some didn't work at all. Some still work on certain days and then can fail miserably on others.

I used a technique called "grounding," and it got me through some very hard nights in the early years. Grounding is something that I thought was my own personal invention until I started researching it and found out that it is a very common and recommended way of handling the rush of emotions in a person's life.

It is simply a focal point that you can grab and place your emotions into at any given time. For years I would wear a rubber band around my ankle. When the rush of emotions would knock on the door of my mind and I started feeling anxious, then I would sit down and flick the rubber band a few times. The reality of the pain of the rubber band snapping against my leg would bring me back to reality. I know that it sounds strange, but it would bring me back down immediately.

I now try to carry a special ink pen with me, a key ring, or a coin in my pocket. When the anxiousness becomes too much to bear, I reach for it and hold it. Rub it. Grab it tight. It worked and still works for me. Other times, throwing a fresh piece of gum in my mouth to chew on will do wonders for my emotional roller coaster.

There are days that I would rush home and turn on *The Andy Griffith Show* on the television. I know my family must have thought that I was crazy (and still do), but during those very bad days, an episode of Andy and Opie would get me through the flashback or unexpected rush of feelings.

Over the years, music has been something that has kept me grounded. Just sitting alone in the office and listening to a meaningful song or playing the piano until my fingers hurt gets me through those floods of overwhelming thoughts, memories, and emotions. When my memories are triggered and become too real, grounding was and is a technique that keeps me in the "now."

I have to force myself to remember that I am not being abused or controlled today. That was in the past.

Today is a day that I control.

Today is a day that I can make a choice to control or allow the past to control me.

It's a choice.

I choose to live in the NOW.

No matter what it takes me to live in the moment, I have to consciously keep that in the front of my mind.

So no matter how much emotional coffee has spilled out all over the floor, take a step back and take a deep breath. Grab ahold of something that means something to you and hang on tight.

Eventually it will stop flowing.

Eventually it will start to slow down and start dripping slower and slower.

And finally the emotions will stop . . . at least for that moment.

You may not believe it now, but they will.

And when they do, smile, reach up, and throw the used coffee grounds in the trash.

And remember to *stay grounded*.

CHAPTER 13

Darkness loves darkness. Darkness not only invades the physical environment in which a person resides but it also tries everything within its power to convince the heart and mind of the person that it is the best place to live.

Darkness can convince the world it brings peace and security and tranquility, when in reality darkness becomes a place where things are hidden and allowed to exist without letting the light shine upon it.

The night comes and goes each and every day, but if darkness has total control of a heart of a person, it will manipulate them to hide the deepest secrets in places where darkness can forever reside.

Places where light isn't allowed to enter.

Darkness loves darkness.

Darkness hates the light.

Where can the darkness cause the most devastating damage?

Inside the deepest and darkest parts of a heart.

CARRYING THE HEAVY LOAD

Trying to start a family and a career in my early twenties was a challenge for me like it is for any young college graduate. The beginning of a new chapter in life has its advantages and disadvantages. I think my mistakes outweighed my accomplishments 10:1.

I quickly realized that relationships, in life and in business, would have a different dimension for me because of my first sixteeen years of abuse. There were so many issues that I was carrying inside of me. So much extra baggage that I thought I needed to drag along with me.

Emotional baggage.

Heavy trunks and crates of hurts.

Pallets of disappointments and low self-esteem that I was determined to keep deep inside me.

Trying to pretend that I wasn't carrying this extra stuff around with me emotionally was about as easy as trying to park an oversized semi-truck trailer in a parking spot designed for a compact car. It just wasn't working. But I kept trying to reposition the baggage and hide the load, day after day, and just hoping that no one would notice.

Did that work? Absolutely not!

The aftermath of abuse during my childhood had a ripple effect throughout so many areas of my life. Obviously, the damage that was done to me while I was being abused both emotionally and physically took its toll, but years later the trauma still had a damaging impact.

My view of relationships and my ability to trust other people were permanently tainted no matter how hard I tried to overcome it. It was as if someone crawled into the inside of my eyes and painted a different shade of reality over what I could see. My entire view of the people and world around me was forever changed.

Friendships were difficult for me because there was always thoughts of the other person hurting me or taking advantage of me no matter what their real intent was. Trust became a big issue and still is a major issue in my life. I often have to work through a process in my mind to allow myself to trust others.

Abuse victims often battle with their view of the world and how they should relate to other people. I, like other victims, found myself isolated or "on an island" away from friends and family.

One thing that I often deal with is that I push people away when I feel they are getting too close. Even when I would be experiencing a bad day and family members or friends would ask how they could help, I would often say that I would want to be left alone. In reality, the last thing I wanted was to be left alone, but I would always push people away.

The emotional baggage can be very confusing and can make personal relationships difficult. When I finally told some family members what my father did to me, their reactions were completely different. Some members of my family totally denied that it ever happened, and from that moment on, we never discussed it again. A few family members completely alienated me and we have never spoken since.

Some family and friends just simply didn't know how to deal with this kind of issue and the relationship became difficult and awkward. Over the years, I have found that simply talking about it and then moving forward was the best solution for me.

I remember telling Mom and her reaction was that of shock and horror, but then she admitted that she knew that Dad had many "demons" inside of him and that he was disturbed sexually. I often wondered if Mom knew or even suspected that I was being abused daily. She said that she didn't and swore that if she had known, she would have probably killed him after discovering the news.

It isn't my place to questions someone's word, but I do feel that there were so many dysfunctional pieces of our home that were out of control. The cloud of darkness can have a strange and powerful effect on those surrounding the actual abuse. Everyone in our home was a victim of my father's darkness in some way. No one escaped without being forever imprinted by my dad's demented and controlling behavior.

After I told my mom, she was never the same. I think the overwhelming emotions took over and then she internally started blaming herself for not protecting me. I also feel that she looked back on all those years and probably noticed that she missed or overlooked many red flags and guilt settled in.

Many abuse victims are scared to even let other people know what they have experienced. I remember going through the gamut of emotions when I finally started letting people know what had happened to me.

Some of the questions that I would ask in my mind included:

"Would anyone believe me?" Remember, my father told me repeatedly through my childhood that no one would ever believe me. He had me totally brainwashed that I would be called a liar.

"What would people think of me if I tell about my abuse?"

"Would people look at me differently if they knew I was abused?"

"Would people still love me?"

"Would my own family reject me or would they accept me?"

The internal battle that raged on for years kept all these secrets secret. I didn't have the answers to those questions so I put all the abuse, all the feelings of the abuse, all the aftermath of the abuse in several emotional storage boxes and locked them in a closet.

After years of feeling that those emotions and memories of abuse were safely locked away, my mind and heart started realizing that I needed to take time and slowly open all those emotional boxes of horror and deal with them one by one.

True healing only comes from facing the issues head on. Healing will never come from burying the hurts and hoping they are never discovered. If you have been hurt or abused, please read those sentences again.

True healing only comes from facing the issues head on.

Unwrap the hurt and find someone that you trust to discuss it with. It is important that you find someone that won't judge you. Someone that will just listen.

Taking the emotional hurts out of these boxes that have been stored away for years can be a very long process, but it is a very important one. Take your time and don't rush through it.

It took me over thirty years to even let people know what had happened. This book is my very personal way of unwrapping those hurts and letting the world know.

Will I get through all the boxes and unwrap all the abuse in these hundred pages or so? Absolutely not! There are still several boxes that may take me a few more years to even work up enough courage to let my family know. There are some instances of my sexual abuse that I really don't even know how to describe, let alone feeling comfortable to share that level of abuse with other people. I feel that one day I will empty those boxes that are back in the far closet of my heart and fully let everything out.

Remember, this is a process. It doesn't happen overnight.

My best advice to those who have been abused is to write your feelings down in a journal. Every thought. Every feeling. Every hurt. Every crazy idea that went through your mind while it was going on and every thought you had about it after. Then find someone that you trust and let them read a few pages of your writing. Just start off with letting them read a few pages, not all of it.

The one thing that I needed to be told, and which no one ever told me was this: I didn't have to handle this alone. So please hear this from me right now and believe me:

YOU DON'T HAVE TO HANDLE THIS ALONE!

No matter how small the hurt is.

No matter how big the abuse is.

Find someone to talk to and start pulling all of those boxes and crates out of the darkest corner of your heart and slowly but deliberately start opening them and unpacking each hurt.

Even the box that you labeled "Fragile." "Handle with care." That box, too.

Find a trusted friend, a recommended counselor, or a respected therapist and start the process. True healing begins with unpacking your hurts, pains, and abuses and letting it all out.

My healing began when I unlocked the door and let some light shine on all those years of pain.

CHAPTER 14

Day after day, week after week, year after year, darkness came and went. Each visit of the night caused more and more havoc in my life.

As darkness was fading to never cause pain or hurt again, a very important confrontation was inevitable.

Without this faceoff, darkness would never leave the room.

It had to happen before darkness gave up its last breath.

The final face to face discussion must happen before . . . darkness dies.

THE DAY
DARKNESS DIED

One of the memories of my father that will forever be etched in my mind was his love for cigarettes. Dad smoked constantly, and every room in our house had more than one ashtray. There were very few times that I can ever remember Dad not having a cigarette in his mouth.

I know there were several cigarette burns on my bedside dresser where he would be smoking and then lay the cigarette down, abuse me, and then pick it back up when he was finished. He always reeked of smoke. I will never get that smell out of my mind.

After all the years of smoking, the cigarettes finally took their toll on Dad's body and he was diagnosed with throat cancer. He eventually ended up having throat surgery that would put him in the hospital for months. I took every opportunity to visit him and be involved in his treatment plans with his doctors and nurses.

This was in the late months of the year 2000 when I was thirty-seven years old, married, and had children. Dad and I never discussed the abuse except on one occasion several years before when I briefly talked to him on the phone and mentioned to him what he did to me. He went totally quiet. It was never discussed again.

Throughout Dad's illnesses, we never talked about the past and only had casual conversations about work, the kids, and how he was feeling. The medical treatments and his sickness were starting to get the best of him physically.

In mid-2001, Dad had another surgery and that was the beginning of the end for him. During the surgery, his lungs collapsed, and because of all the years of smoking, they weren't able to rebound back. He was in a medically induced coma for several months.

I visited him often, and on one of those occasions in late December of 2001, I had a very long and one-sided conversation with him. During that discussion, I expressed to him all the hurt and pain that he had caused me.

I will never forget that day. He was attached to a breathing machine that was keeping him alive. His hands and face were swollen because of all the illness in his body. I leaned over his bed and whispered into his ear, "Dad, I remember each night that you came into my room. You destroyed my childhood."

I went into detail about many of those nights. I was very graphic and described to him exactly what he did to me.

"You remember those nights you invited your friends to abuse me, too?" I continued. "I remember every one of their faces and every one of their names."

I went on for a very long time, even though he couldn't talk even if he wanted to. It was very important to me to let it all out. Finally.

I told him more and more about all of those nights and all of the things that he did to me. I stopped and cried several times during. The nurse interrupted a couple of times to silence a beeping machine or to check his vitals.

Being determined in my heart to finish this conversation, I continued no matter how many times I was interrupted.

After about thirty or forty minutes, I finally said, "Dad, I want you to know something."

"Even though you treated me like trash, I love you," I whispered.

"Something else that I want you to know, I will never tell anyone about this until Mom dies and then I will let the whole world know," I said.

"And one last thing, I forgive you," I concluded. Immediately when I said those words, something happened inside my mind and my body. There was a sense of letting a huge weight off of my back.

I have to be honest, it took years and years to completely forgive him and maybe I still haven't 100 percent, but there was a very definite emotional release when I uttered those words: "I forgive you."

We can have a debate every day for the next two years about whether or not a patient who is in a medically induced coma can hear or even comprehend a discussion of this magnitude. Let me tell you this, when I finished my talk with him, I leaned back up from his ear and looked at his face and there were tears flowing down both sides of his face onto his pillow.

That was my confirmation that he heard me. Dad never acknowledged abusing me or ever asked me to forgive him. The forgiveness I offered my dad that day wasn't for his benefit anyway. It was for mine.

I had to try to forgive. Anger was ravaging my mind, my peace, and my insides. A famous quote that lots of people claim to have authored, goes like this: "Unforgiveness is like drinking poison and expecting the other person to die." If you get nothing more out of this book than that understanding, it was worth it all.

For me, starting to attempt to forgive my father and to at least utter those words, "I forgive you" gave me a great sense of peace. I left a thousand-pound weight in that hospital room that day after that conversation.

This conversation came twenty-one years after the sexual abuse had ceased. I had desperately wanted to have this confrontation many years prior to this day but never had the courage to do it. Even though he didn't say a word and maybe couldn't understand a word that I was saying to him, to me there was a very important "release." Freedom from a prison that was not only created by my dad but a cell that I wouldn't allow myself to be released from because of unforgiveness in my heart.

Thousands of abuse victims battle inner demons of unforgiveness and place themselves in a debate of attempting to forgive their abuser or not. Just because an attempt of forgiveness is offered to the offender that doesn't excuse their terrible behavior. Forgiveness just prevents their horrendous actions from continuing to destroy your heart and mind and peace.

The forgiveness that I started offering to my dad in that hospital room on that day was the beginning of a long journey back to real freedom.

Real freedom.

Real joy.

Real peace.

I want to be brutally honest, there were days that I wanted to reach over and unplug my father's life support machine because of my anger and pain.

But on this day instead of thinking about taking his life away from him, I decided to reach out and take my life back. Forgiveness was the beginning of me taking my life back. I will never forget that one-sided conversation and I am forever thankful that I said those words, "I forgive you."

A few weeks later, on January 9, 2002, my father died.

On that day, the darkness that shattered my life gave up his final breath.

Finally, darkness was dead.

CHAPTER 15

The absence of darkness doesn't necessarily mean that light takes over and immediately shines through.

The damaging effects of what happened during the night aren't lessened just because the darkness is gone.

But when the darkness disappears, it gives the opportunity for the light to finally break through. The clouds can begin to be pushed away, one at a time, and the new dawn can start to come into view.

COLD DAY
IN JANUARY 2002

On Friday, January 11, 2002, at exactly 10 AM, a professionally dressed funeral director escorted me up to an old wooden lectern positioned a few feet from the head of my father's casket. A few brief moments later the piped-in music faded and I stood there in front of family, friends, and neighbors and began to speak.

No one sitting in the chapel of that funeral home on that cold and brisk morning had any idea what was lying in front of them in that over-priced casket. To them, it was the body of a loving husband, a caring father, a compassionate grandfather, a wonderful brother, or a dependable friend.

To me, it was the shell of an abusing, overbearing, controlling, and manipulative monster. But this wasn't the day to declare to the world what this man had done to me over the years. So I said all of the proper things that the family and friends expected me to say as I gave the eulogy at the funeral.

I spoke words of comfort to those sitting there and I even sang a song to help ease their emotional pain. Interestingly, the song I chose to sing was called "No More Night." I never gave one clue to anyone there that this was the ending of a sixty-seven-year-old man's life but also the ending of a chapter of my life that he had completely destroyed.

When the service was over and all the people filed by for their final viewing of my dad's body, I stood there alone with the funeral director and looked down at his overly cosmetized face and paused for a moment.

Nothing dramatic; I just took in the moment.

I placed my hand on his rigid and cold hands and patted them.

Looking over at the funeral director, I said, "Okay, I'm ready." I stepped back and they closed the lid of his casket.

"Don't forget to lock the lid," I added. For some symbolic reason, I wanted to be sure that there was no way that lid would ever be opened again.

About forty-five minutes later, we left the cemetery and the shell of the body that caused so much pain and damage to my mind, my body, and my life. That day was very unusual and profound as I experienced rushes of emotions and memories.

New memories came rushing into my mind and then quickly left. I was overwhelmed with stress and anxiety, and then, in a split second, I had a sense of calmness and exhilaration. I honestly didn't know how to respond. I wanted to cry and then I wanted to laugh. I was a complete mixed bag of feelings.

But one thing I did know, the nightmare was officially over. It was buried six feet under.

Wouldn't life be so great if you could just package up all the bad memories, awful experiences, heartaches, and pain in an overpriced box and bury them forever? Life doesn't work that way.

Even though the darkness had died in my life, the real events engraved in my mind and heart wouldn't fade from my memory. The internal process of dealing with the years of abuse and darkness had to be addressed.

There were so many different challenges that I was facing and that many abuse victims face. The list of issues includes fears, flashbacks, nightmares, obsessive compulsive disorder, post-traumatic stress disorder, low self-esteem, and self harm, and that is just the tip of the iceberg.

The experience of dealing with my dad's death and funeral brought thousands of bad memories and thoughts in my mind. During those few months around his death and after, my emotional issues seemed to increase and my flashbacks and nightmares reeoccurred more often than the previous ten years. Just when I thought that I had completely silenced the fears and nightmares, they returned with a vengeance.

One of the most impactful things that I ever did in helping myself deal with my past was to finally, after all of the years, to tell someone.

I honestly never thought that I would be able to tell anyone what had happened to me. Never. But one day I shared one page of my journey with someone, and it was the beginning of the darkness breaking away.

There was something very special in feeling the freedom to express my experience, although it was only one instance. I remember feeling a certain amount of weight being lifted from inside my heart.

It felt good.

There was something that came to my mind immediately after I revealed my abuse. It was a moment of relief but also discovery. The relief came from sharing my pain. The discovery came from the reality that I wasn't shunned or doubted. I felt accepted and valued, and for the first time in my life, I knew that I was going to be alright.

This was a major decision in my life. A shift from, "The Sound of Silence" as my theme song to Barry Manilow's "I Made It Through the Rain" as my new ballad. Not being ashamed of my past was something that became very important to me.

The words to the new song in my life became real.

> *"We dreamers have our ways*
> *Of facing rainy days*
> *And somehow we survive . . ."*

It was a small step for me but also a huge leap. Darkness couldn't keep me silent anymore. It could not control or manipulate my mind and convince me that no one cared and no one would believe me.

I had left that old life buried in the ground of a cemetery on that cold winter day in January of 2002.

CHAPTER 16

Darkness convinces the world that it can't be controlled.

The only way to fight off the depth of the night is to allow light into the heart.

MY BATTLE FOR CONTROL

Now that my father had passed away, I thought that my life would immediately start showing signs of emotional improvement, but in reality, that's when my negative emotions became more and more internalized.

For as long as I can remember, I had some signs of obsessive compulsive disorder (OCD), but I overlooked it as nothing to be concerned with. For instance, I always washed my hands or sanitized my hands much more than anyone else around me. As a child, I thought it was because of the abuse and not being able to remove the smell of my father off of my body.

The older I got, the more obsessive I became with little things that shouldn't have mattered, but caused me great inner pain when I experienced them. Not only did I have an issue with washing my hands but I wouldn't want to touch my food with my hands. I constantly used a knife and a fork to eat pizza, cheeseburgers and fries, and common "finger foods."

To a general observer, it would seem that I was having issues getting food, grease, or debris on my hands, but in my mind, there was a much more serious issue. In my mind, my hands were never clean enough to touch the food and thus I wanted to use a fork. But one of the craziest things is that I could drop a fork or knife on the floor and not have an issue at all with picking it up and declaring the three-second rule and continue using it.

Germs weren't the major cause of my emotional stress. The mental dilemma was *my* germs had the ability to contaminate the food that I was getting ready to eat and I didn't want that to happen.

Soon after my father died, I started noticing a new and disturbing issue that I was battling internally that quickly became some heavy emotional baggage. I would become overly concerned with particular daily events in my life that started taking over my mental ability to handle them. Simple tasks.

For instance:

- Getting up at the exact same time every morning.
- Leaving the house to go to work at the same time.
- Arriving at work at the very same minute each day.
- Using the same amount of steps to get to my car.
- Never ordering anything different at restaurants.
- Not allowing myself to be late for an appointment.
- Becoming very frustrated when others weren't as concerned with their tardiness.

- Having to have everything on my desk in exact order at all times.
- Being bothered when others would move something out of place.

The list could go on and on, but that gives you a general idea of many of the issues that I was becoming obsessed with shortly after my dad died. These issues were always present throughout my life, but it seemed that after the funeral the issues started to accelerate. The increased velocity started to take over any kind of normalcy or peace. The OCD was starting to take over.

Even to this day, I still deal with OCD in my life, but I try not to let it control me as I have in the past. It honestly is a daily battle that some days I win and some days I come in a close second place.

A casual observer may not even notice anything from the outside. But inside my mind, the gears, pistons, and motors were starting to rev up to a speed that was totally out of control.

It felt like mentally I was driving a sports car down a very steep hill full of curves and sharp turns and my foot continued to accelerate, causing the car to spin totally out of control. No matter what I tried to do to slow my mind down, nothing helped. Inside my head, I was totally out of control.

Scenes of the abuse would flash through my mind over and over again throughout the day and night.

The only way I felt any kind of control was when I took control of the little things that were in front of me. For instance, if I would wake up at 3:38 each morning on the digital clock, then all was well. But if I would oversleep to 3:40, my entire day would be shot. During those times of stress my mind would see scenes of my father's face or feel his hands on the back of my head.

If I could leave my front door and make it to my car in exactly seventeen steps, then all was well. But if I forgot something in the house and had to go back and get it, then the morning would immediately become unbearable because I failed to control that moment in my day. My mind would quickly be filled with scenes of being in the shower with my father or him kissing my chest or some other abuse.

I would deliberately show up for appointments twenty or thirty minutes early just so I would have total control of my environment. If traffic caused me to be a few minutes later than my comfort zone allowed, my internal mental engine would whirl out of control.

During all of these instances, I never revealed to anyone what was going on inside of my mind. I would simply internalize all of the anguish and the stress. It was as if now my emotional sports car was gaining speed while the engine was low on engine oil. The motor was getting overheated more and more each day.

I created many ways to temporarily deal with my own personal issues with OCD:

- I would set out all of my clothes and all of my things needed the night before to reduce the chance of anything delaying my morning routine.

- I tried to find an occupation that focused on precision and important deadlines. I relied on my obsessiveness to make sure each and every detail was in order and done on time. I also found that channeling this internal drive in a positive way made me very successful in the work environment.

- I tried not to put myself in situations that would upset the normal flow of my day. So going to work extra early seemed to work as it eliminated the need to worry about traffic that would cause me undue stress.

But these were just temporary fixes for a much larger problem. It was like I was putting a Band-Aid on the chest of a gunshot victim.

Eventually, the toll mentally, physically, and emotionally had to give way; the engine was getting overheated and the warning lights were flashing red.

In January 2010, I had open-heart surgery to repair a heart valve that had gone bad. Of course, the heart surgeon would probably never testify that all my emotional stresses caused my heart to finally start becoming overworked. But personally I think that is exactly what happened. I do remember the heart surgeon telling me there was no medical reason that appears to have caused my heart valve to deteriorate. Years later, I discovered adverse childhood experiences (ACEs) research that explains early childhood trauma can have major health consequences later in life. This is life-changing information that everyone should be aware of. My engine just couldn't take anymore.

Many sexual abuse victims deal with the issues of obsessive compulsive disorder and also post-traumatic stress disorder. It is of major importance that when the emotional and mental spirals are starting that you seek immediate help.

I tried for years to handle all of the stress and flashbacks and OCD issues alone, and I found that just didn't work. In order for emotional healing to start, I had to ask others for support. I had to trust again and reach out to get help.

I found that letting other people know my story, my past abuse, and my fears and failures has helped me realize that darkness doesn't have to always be the end result.

I learned over the years that the darkest nights produce the brightest stars.

CHAPTER 17

Darkness is liar. It strives to claim authority and control by the mere suggestion of its existence.

Darkness is a grand manipulator. It relies on the fear of those experiencing it to continue its reign. It convinces you that those things that happen while in the darkness somehow give it power.

In reality, darkness is powerless.

THE REAL IMAGE IN
THE MIRROR

I n this chapter I want to let you see something that causes me daily pain even after almost thirty years of the abuse ceasing in my life.

Even though the abuse has stopped physically in my life, the daily reminders, thoughts, and emotions continue to ripple through my heart and mind. There are good days, but there are still some bad days.

Even though I don't want to be a victim any longer, it still lingers in my mind.

Every single day.

My daily worst enemy now is my mirror. I wake up and stumble in to the bathroom and start my daily routine. I shave and then wash my face and then the worst part of my day occurs: looking into the mirror.

What I see each morning looking back at me totally disgusts me. The image of my face is something that I wish I could change. Even though I am very aware that I have been created by a God that has made me very special and unique, there are still emotions inside me that won't allow me to see anything positive in the morning mirror.

The constant years of abuse warped my internal view of what I see through my eyes when looking at myself. My self-esteem is something that I have to constantly work on 24/7, 365 days of the year.

I know that I am not the only person who has this issue. A child being exposed to all those years of abuse and having a father spew nasty, negative, and degrading things will forever damage and scar a young child's heart. Then, while I was an impressionable teenager, my father constantly made humiliating comments to me, which is truly hard to overcome.

Sometimes I wish that I could just simply hit an internal "delete" or "erase" button and things would simply go away inside my mind. But, unfortunately, each time I reach for those buttons, the volume is turned up and the button that ends up being hit is the "repeat" button. Over and over again.

Not to overshadow the drastic effects that physical abuse can have on a life, but the emotional effects can often be much more long-lasting. Even though my body still has physical scars on it from the sexual abuse it endured, those have healed over and I don't think about them daily. The emotional damage is something that can't be treated with a Band-Aid and some salve, it goes much deeper than that. These emotional scars are constantly in my mind, life, and heart.

My issue with low self-esteem is something that I do not face alone. Many abuse victims, battered spouses, and neglected children deal with this ever-present emotion daily. They feel that their value is somewhat diminished because of the crisis that they went through.

My father used this tool to control me in my thinking. He convinced me that no one would want anything to do with me because I was damaged goods. He spent hour after hour, day after day, training my mind that no one but him could love me and no one could be trusted.

One day I plan to go deeper into all of the abuses that I haven't had the courage to deal with. I'm not ready to unlock those memories yet. It still hurts too much. It would take volumes and volumes of books to capture all the instances and all the emotional issues I have battled for the last three decades—some successful, some not so successful. But I am a work in progress. I continue to strive for complete healing.

I have come too far now to allow myself to revert back to my old ways of coping, my safety zone. I have to keep opening those painful memories in order to continue my journey toward healing. I have learned there is no timeframe I have to follow. As long as I am moving forward day by day, I am progressing.

The real truth is, no matter what I see looking back at me in the bathroom mirror, there is someone in there that is very special.

There is someone in that mirror that has value and worth.

There is someone in that mirror that didn't cause this to happen. It wasn't my fault that I was abused.

There is someone in that mirror that can help other people.

There is someone in that mirror that can love and be loved unconditionally.

There is someone in that mirror that has a past, but doesn't have to be a prisoner of that past.

There is someone in that mirror that has experienced the darkness, but doesn't have to be controlled by it anymore.

I have discovered that I am not defined by my past.

If you don't get anything else from this book, please read the next few lines slowly and carefully:

No matter what situation you have endured and gone through in your life.

Sexual abuse.

Rape.

Battered by a spouse.

Divorce.

Failure.

Betrayal by your best friend.

Wrongly accused.

Go look in the mirror and take a deep breath.

You are someone that is very special.

You are someone that has great value and worth.

You are not to blame for what happened to you.

You do not have to be a prisoner of the past any longer.

You do not have to be controlled by the darkness anymore.

Today is the day to make a life-changing decision to fight back.

Today is the day to take back control of your life again.

Today is the day to start heading in the direction of your personal and inner healing.

It is a long journey, but a journey that is worth the work and effort.

You can do this, too.

Granted, the hardest step is the first one, but along with that step, you are also beginning your journey toward healing. I want to help you with that. I am a safe place for you to begin telling *your* story.

This is not your fault. You are not alone.

Today is the day to start
SHATTERING YOUR DARKNESS.

CONCLUSION

There are so many more stories, events, and memories that I will eventually share, possibly in the next book. Some of the memories are still locked away in secret places of my heart that I haven't built up enough courage yet to open up. But this is the beginning of the journey to reach the full potential of what life has to offer.

Let me encourage you that no matter what pain you have experienced in life, there is always a way to turn each and every negative event into something that can be used to help someone else. My greatest therapy is not only letting many of the memories out of my heart by penning this book, but realizing that when I speak of my hurts, I see the hundreds and thousands of people's lives that have been changed for the better because of it.

As each person talks to me after a presentation or emails me after reading the book, it brings with it a ray of light. Light that drives away another piece of the darkness. This can happen to you, too. I just know it. Allow all the darkness that you and I have walked through become an eternal light that will help lead others through their own private pain and dark times. You have the strength inside of you to walk through your darkness so one day you may help others eventually see the light in their own lives.

Take the first step of your journey today toward the light and experience the hope that is waiting for each of us.

APPENDIX 1

EDUCATION AND SHARING YOUR
STORY ARE THE KEYS

Sexual abuse does not discriminate. It is not bound by race, creed, age, religious beliefs, economic class, profession, or location. The silence of victims does not diminish the reality that physical, emotional, and psychological abuse continues to happen every single day all over the world and has since the beginning of time.

When we hear of child abuse, we tend to think of the young child. I believe the number of adult survivors of childhood abuse is far greater than any of us can imagine. It may be your own mother, father, best friend, pastor, or counselor, and the list goes on and on. It is time they, too, are given the encouragement they need to take that first

step toward releasing their past and begin their own journey of healing. I am committed to telling my story with
raw honesty—my whole story—not just the parts society
deems acceptable. Abuse is not pretty. Horrific things do
happen to innocent people.

One of the most amazing discoveries that I have
learned about, and I would like to introduce to you, is the
educational research of Adverse Childhood Experiences
(ACEs). This unbelievable research has been around for
many years, but is just now starting to get the recognition
and visibility that is deserves. Once I started to look into
this information, it gave me a clearer understanding of
what was actually happening to me in my mental, physical,
emotional, spiritual, and relational being. It was literally
life-changing.

I had spent hour after hour in therapy digging into my
past abuse and the overwhelming impact that it still had
on me decades later. It seemed that retelling the hurts and
pains of my childhood trauma to different therapists, counselors, and psychiatrists only helped to a certain degree; it
didn't come full circle until I discovered the ACEs impact.

This life-changing information is beneficial to each person that has been affected by any type of trauma, whether
it was a single episode or years of abuse. Trauma is trauma.
Pain is pain. Ignorance says to ignore it and just "move on

and get over it." But, believe me, I have learned this the hard way: Trauma and pain need to be addressed, faced, and dealt with. Once I found the ACEs research and the ACEs resilience research, it changed my life.

If only I had learned about this ground-breaking information years before, my life might not have been so unsettled and fragmented. I would have been a much better husband, father, employee, and friend to so many people. One of the tragic discoveries that I made is what effects ACEs and toxic stress can have on a person, and how they are passed on to generation after generation.

Here is a golden nugget of truth: Abuse victims aren't suffering alone in the pain and aftermath. It affects each person that is in their life. It has a lasting impact on those surrounding them, their family inner-circle, their friends, and associates.

Because of the importance of the informational impact that ACEs has had on my recovery, I want to spend as much of my life that I have left to help spread the word about this amazing research. This needs to be taught to parents, counselors, schools, physicians, therapists, clergy, and advocacy centers. We need legislation that encourages our communities to have the education, funds, and support it deserves to make sure that all races, economical classes, and creeds have equal access to this vital information and training. Education is the key. Now is the time to get the information out to the masses.

My next book, *Overcoming the Darkness,* is going to dive into this subject in greater depth and detail. But I would highly recommend that you start looking into this research by visiting *www.acesconnection.com*. You will find a wealth of information and a caring community waiting to assist you. I have found the ACEs Connection world to be a safe and welcoming circle of friends and I am sure you will, too.

Sharing your story is another major step for you find solace inside a troubled and hurt heart. We have developed many resources to offer our help in creating a safe environment for people to confidentially share their stories and receive counseling. We have also created a platform to educate and train parents, teachers, medical professionals, church groups, and communities of the potential adult/child abuse victims among them. Our resources will provide educational tools that can be used to recognize potential abuse victims and train them on the proper techniques and resources to provide assistance.

If you would like more information about staff trainings, abuse seminars, "Shattered by the Darkness" seminars, motivational speaking engagements or additional resources please contact us at: *www.shatteredbythedarkness.com*.

Please reach out to me and I will do everything in my

ability to respond to you and take time to listen. We are all in this together. *You are not alone*. Remember that. The only way to make this world a better place is to look around each of us and reach out and help, assist, comfort, and raise each other up and teach the next generation that caring for others is a life principle for all.

You may be just the ray of light that someone else needs to encourage them to break through their darkness that they have hidden for years, too.

APPENDIX 2

THE TRUE LIGHT

I deliberately placed this at the very back of the book, but please don't assume it is because of the lack of importance of these words. I wanted the book to explain my abuse but I feel it is also important to reveal the anchor that kept me sane.

My Uncle Ray and Aunt Dorothy were major influences in my life. I briefly spoke of them in the early chapters. They, along with my Grandma Lucille, always were willing to come by each Sunday morning and take me to church. Through their weekly commitments to make sure I went to church, I was introduced to my Lord and Savior, Jesus Christ.

Because I had given my heart and life to Jesus at a very early age, He gave me an inner strength to deal with my daily abuse. It's hard to explain, but there was an internal strength that kept me strong on the inside, while I was experiencing an overwhelming amount of issues and problems along the way.

I remember after I committed my life to Christ and was baptized, Uncle Ray and Aunt Dorothy gave me a little New Testament Bible that had a picture of Jesus on the front with a small boy on His lap and children all around Him smiling. As a very small child, I stared at that Bible cover for hours believing that I was that little child on Jesus' lap. I kept trusting that He was going to get me through this horrific nightmare.

And He did!

I wore that Bible out carrying it around with me. It was always on my bedroom dresser as a child and I spent hours putting myself on the lap of Jesus in my mind. Oh, how I wish I had that Bible today.

Church became very important to me and I really enjoyed going and eventually because of my involvement, Mom and Dad started going, too. I sometimes think that dad started coming to keep a close eye on me, because he was never happy to go. He frequently tried to discourage me in getting involved with the church activities.

Week after week, I would sit there in the second to the last pew of that little old country church next to my dad with his arm around me, listening to sermon after sermon realizing that I was sitting next to the evil that the preacher was talking about. To be brutally honest, that messed with my mind a lot.

My faith became very important to me, and it truly was the anchor that kept me grounded during those violent storms. It remains the foundation of truth and stability in my life today. Yes, I experienced many years of darkness but I was never alone. He was holding my hand every step of the way.

Jesus became and still is the True Light in my life and without Him I am convinced I would not have made it. He was always there in the middle of my dark nights providing me security and reassurance that I would survive.

John 8:12 "I am the light of the world. Whoever follows Me will never walk in darkness, but will have the light of life." (NIV)

Jesus, the True Light.